PRAYER
CHANGES
THINGS

PRAYER CHANGES THINGS

CHARLES L. ALLEN

Fleming H. Revell
A Division of Baker Book House Co
Grand Rapids, Michigan 49516

© 1964, 2003 by Charles Livingstone Allen

Published by Fleming H. Revell
a division of Baker Book House Company
P.O Box 6287, Grand Rapids, MI 49516-6287
www.bakerbooks.com

Second printing, May 2004

Printed in the United States of America

Library of Congress Cataloging-in-Publication Data
Allen, Charles Livingstone, 1913–
    Prayer changes things / Charles L. Allen.
        p.   cm.
    ISBN 0-8007-5906-0
    1. Christian life—Methodist authors. I. Title.
BV4501.3.A45 2004
248.3'2—dc22   2003017190

CONTENTS

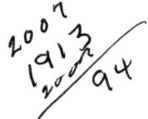

WHAT I BELIEVE PRAYER IS

I am a minister of the Lord and have been pretty much all of my life, a calling I have found to be very fulfilling. Of course, we preachers do tend to talk a lot. But I never imagined in the early days that I would write anything of any substance, much less whole books. To think that those books would be in print for decades and would minister to people all over the world . . . well, that's almost too much for this ordinary fellow to imagine. But it happened.

The book you hold in your hands is an extension of two of my previous books—*God's Psychiatry* and *All Things Are Possible Through Prayer*—and I am pleased to introduce readers to this new edition of *Prayer Changes Things*. It was forty years ago when Fleming H. Revell first published it, and for me, it's been forty years of being humbled by the knowledge that God has used this book to bring readers closer to Him through a stronger, more vibrant prayer life. I believe that God has used this book in particular to help the hurting and the fearful be assured that God is a constant friend—a friend who truly wants them to talk to Him.

As Christians, we are encouraged to pray without ceasing. I've devoted much of my writing to that very idea, that praying to God is the foundation in the everyday walk of the believer. But maybe you think that kind of foundation is for other people. Maybe you feel alone or ineffective, and you aren't certain God is there for you. Maybe these frightening times have you over a barrel. Maybe you believe prayer is for people who are more spiritual, a word we toss around pretty carelessly these days.

Well, I can guarantee you that God is there. He is nearby, and He wants to hear from you. That's what *Prayer Changes Things* is about—communicating with the God who cares about you and your life, the God who cherishes the very sound of your voice.

The idea of prayer may seem like a big concept to you, even too big to understand. So I've tried to break it down into simple actions in these pages. I've included Scripture you can savor and handy axioms to remember. I've tried to turn ideas into food for thought in small enough portions that you can pick up the book anywhere, anytime, and be fed.

I am grateful that God has let me live these many years to see the fruits of my labors. And I am especially grateful to know that you, the reader, or someone you love, may be helped by the reading of this book. It is my sincere hope that you find yourself drawing closer to your Creator who loves you very much. I believe you will indeed find that prayer changes things in ways you never before imagined. May God bless you in your endeavors.

Charles L. Allen
Houston, Texas
2003

1

FIVE QUESTIONS ABOUT PRAYER

Often people write or speak to me of problems for which I just do not know the answers. In such cases I admit that I do not know how to advise him or her, but I suggest that we enter into a compact together to pray about it. Many times, as a result of our prayers, problems have been solved.

One man, however, in response to my prayer suggestion, wrote back a difficult letter. "Before I agree to pray," he wrote, "answer the following five questions: What is prayer? Can anybody pray? Can you prove the value of prayer? How does one pray? What results can I expect from prayer?" How would you answer those questions? Let's take them one at a time:

What Is Prayer?

What is prayer? In a very fine speech that I heard one night, a scientist was explaining the difference between "black magic" and "white magic." Black magic is using the forces of evil for one's own benefit. White magic is using the forces of good for one's own benefit. He went on to explain that many people think of religion as something they can use. Many people think of prayer merely as white magic.

Prayer is not magic. Prayer is within the laws of the universe, and the spiritual laws of the universe are as certain and sure as are the physical laws. Physical and spiritual laws work together; they are never in conflict. As Pierhal states it, "Although prayer is supernatural, it is not anti-natural."

Prayer is never a substitute for effort. A certain schoolboy failed in his examinations. He was very much surprised. When the teacher inquired how much he had studied, he replied, "I did not study at all. I thought that if you asked God to help you, that was all you had to do."

On the other hand, prayer is something beyond our efforts. On the night of July 10, 1943, General Dwight D. Eisenhower watched the vast armada of three thousand ships sailing across from Malta to the shores of Sicily for a great battle. The general saluted his heroic men and then bowed his head in prayer. To an officer beside him, Eisenhower explained, "There comes a time when you've used your brains, your training, your technical skill, and the die is cast and the events are in the hands of God, and there you have to leave them."

Prayer is need finding a voice—embarrassment seeking relief—a friend in search of a Friend—knocking on a barred door—reaching out through the darkness. Prayer is speaking or thinking or feeling with the belief that there is Somebody who hears and who cares and who will respond. Prayer is a means of contact with God. Prayer is opening our lives to the purposes of God.

Prayer is not a method of using God; rather prayer is a means of reporting for duty to God.

Can Anybody Pray?

Can anybody pray? The answer is, everybody can and does pray. Some people think they are self-sufficient and do not need help. Some people scoff at the value of prayer, calling it a silly waste of time. Some people lack faith; others are ashamed to face God in prayer because of some sin; some are afraid to pray because they do not want God telling them what to do.

But at one time or another, in one kind of crisis or another, everybody prays. Need becomes stronger than doubt, and sometimes we will turn to God in spite of ourselves. There is a hidden hunger of man's spiritual self that cries out to be satisfied. Sooner or later that hidden hunger asserts itself and makes its demands felt. It is as Victor Hugo said, "There are times in a man's life when, regardless of the attitude of the body, the soul is on its knees in prayer."

Can You Prove the Value of Prayer?

Can you prove the value of prayer? By various tests, many have sought to demonstrate that prayer gets results. But I have never been too interested in such experiments. I am not sure that prayer values can be proved, but certainly they can be known. There is a difference.

In fact, anyone who sincerely prays is himself a proof of prayer.

About prayer, Lincoln once said: "I have had so many evidences of His direction, so many instances of times when I have been controlled by some other power than my own will, that I cannot doubt that this power comes from God. I frequently see my way clear to a decision when I am conscious that I have not sufficient facts on which to found it. I am satisfied that, when the Almighty wants me to do, or not to do, a particular thing, He finds a way of letting me know. I talk to God and when I do my mind seems relieved and a way is suggested." I doubt if Lincoln ever tried to prove the value of prayer—but he knew it.

How Does One Pray?

How does one pray? Late one night my doorbell rang. When I opened the door I found a man standing there. He said, "Something happened to me tonight that caused me to want to pray. But I have never prayed in my life and I do not know how. I don't want you to pray for me—I want you to teach me how to pray for myself." We talked for a while, and I found he had never been to church except for a few times when he was a child. He had never read the Bible. I asked if he knew the Lord's Prayer. He asked, "What is that?"

I told him about Jesus' disciples asking Him to teach them to pray. In response, He gave them a short prayer. I gave my visitor a New Testament and marked the place. I told him that every time he wanted to pray he should get down on his knees, open the Testament, and read that prayer aloud. He said he would do that, and he was deeply in earnest. As a result, that man had a really remarkable religious experience and has developed a wonderful faith.

The best way I know to learn to pray is to learn the Lord's Prayer by heart. It is easy to commit the Lord's Prayer to memory; it takes time and persistence to learn it by heart. But when those words that Jesus gave come out of our own hearts, then we are truly praying.

What Results Can I Expect from Prayer?

What results can I expect from prayer? Some years ago four people who knew much about prayer joined together in forming a declaration. They were George Washington Carver, Glenn Frank, Rufus Jones, and Muriel Lester. They wrote:

> Sometimes a bridge falls, but that does not mean that the law of gravity has failed. Sometimes lines are short-circuited, but that does not mean that the law of electricity has failed. And sometimes a disciple betrays his Lord, but that does not mean that the law of love has failed. Sometimes a prayer is not answered, but that does not mean that the power of prayer has failed. The scientist does not quit when the lights are short-circuited, nor when the bridge falls. Then why should we? Just think of what would happen if all church people united in prayer with as great faith in the laws of God as scientists have in the laws of nature.
>
> Science is showing us that the smaller and more invisible a thing is, the more powerful it is. Pasteur proved to an unbelieving world that bacteria ten thousand times smaller than a flea could kill a man. Physicists are proving that the tiny cosmic ray is far more potent and penetrating than the visible sun ray. Radio operators

are proving that the shortwave length carries a message farther than the long-wave length. And love is invisible, but all-powerful love is more potent and penetrating than cannons, submarines or airplanes ever can be. Prayer in the inner room, invisible to the eyes of men, is still as potent as in the days when Jesus said, "Pray to thy Father who is in secret and thy Father who seeth in secret shall reward you openly."

George Meredith said, "Who riseth from prayer a better man, his prayer is answered." That is really the best result of prayer, but prayer brings definite and tangible results. However, we must keep in mind that we ourselves must become part of the answer.

Here is an illustration: A poor man who lived in the country had an accident and broke his leg. That meant he was laid up for a long while, unable to work. His family was large and needed help. Someone got up a prayer meeting at the church to pray for this family. While the people were praying and asking God to help the family, there was a loud knock on the door of their home. Someone tiptoed to the door, opened it, and there stood a young farm boy who said, "My dad could not attend the prayer meeting tonight, so he just sent his prayers in a wagon." And there was the wagon loaded with potatoes, meat, apples, and other things from the farm. This was an instance where prayers were loaded in a wagon.

As I said, we must become part of the answer to our prayers, but only part. God adds to our abilities, opportunities, and resources whatever is needed and is right to bring about the full answer. It is as Tennyson said,

More things are wrought by prayer
Than this world dreams of. . . .

2

IS GOD FAIR?

Is God fair? The psalmist said, "The judgments of the Lord are true and righteous altogether" (19:9). Is that true? Then what about the babies who are born with physical deformities? How about two mothers who pray for their sons? It often seems that the prayer of one is answered while the other goes unheard.

What says the farmer who lost everything because of a prolonged drought, while refreshing rains fell on the land of another? What about an innocent child who has to suffer because of the sins of his parents? Why does a good man die at forty years of age while one who is a menace to society enjoys good health? Why would a fair God permit a cunning scoundrel to become rich and live in luxury, while some honest, good man meets defeat at every turn?

If God were put on trial, it would be easy to make a case against His fairness. A great horde of witnesses could be brought into court by the prosecution. If I were the attorney for the defense, I would begin with evidence from God's own Word, the Holy Bible. Through the centuries we have used that Book in arriving at a verdict about God. In my defense of the fairness of God, I would make four points.

Man's Disobedience

Turn to the very first chapter of the Bible and you will see that God made a perfect world, and that sin and trouble, pain and death, came in against His holy will. In the creation He saved His noblest work until last, when He made man. To man He gave the ability to think, to determine his own life, the right to choose, the majesty of a free will. But it was a dangerous chance God took. It meant that man could choose evil instead of good; he could obey God or rebel against Him.

Then we read of man's tragic disobedience, which was the beginning of all his troubles. God could have safeguarded man by denying him freedom, but then He would have had to settle for less than a man. The blame for man's troubles must be put on man himself.

Once a little boy pushed his playmate into a ditch, hit him with a rock, and spat in his face. His mother scolded him and said that he should not let Satan cause him to treat his friend that way. The little boy replied, "Mother, Satan did tell me to push him in the ditch and hit him with the rock, but spitting in his face was my own idea."

Well, wasn't it all the little boy's idea? And through the centuries, haven't most of man's troubles come because he has chosen evil instead of good? "Whatsoever a man soweth, that shall he also reap" (Gal. 6:7). Also, the Bible says that the iniquity of the father shall be visited upon the children and the children's children for generations (Exod. 34:7). This is only part of the answer, but it is a part.

A child is run over by a car and killed. Someone piously says, "It was the will of God." But was it? It is comforting to believe that God wanted that child, but it is bad to comfort ourselves at the expense of God's character.

Leslie Weatherhead speaks of God's intentional will, His circumstantial will, and His ultimate will. God intends good for every one of His children. But God also gave man a free will because He wanted men instead of mere puppets or robots. That involved a risk on God's part. It means He must allow some things to happen that He did not intend. But we can be sure of God's final victory. Nothing can ultimately defeat His will.

It has been well said, "Reserve your judgment against God. If time does not set you to singing, eternity will." Certainly God is not limited to the short span of this life for the accomplishing of His purposes. "Now we see through a glass, darkly" (1 Cor. 13:12), said St. Paul, and much happens that we do not understand.

Justice Triumphs

In considering whether or not God is fair, a second point to keep in mind is that justice triumphs more often than we think. There are compensations and rewards for the right, and there are punishments and defeats for the wrong. "Though the mills of God grind slowly," they do grind.

One trouble with us is that we measure the justice and fairness of God by the wrong things. Living in a fine house, having money in the bank, high honors, and even good health are not in themselves blessings; one may have those things and much more and also have an uneasy conscience, a restless heart, and a hatred of self. At one period in his life David cried out, "Day and night thy hand was heavy upon me" (Ps. 32:4). He had power and wealth, but he was miserable.

Justice has a way of coming out on top. God so made the world to work that a man gets what is coming to him. A quick glance might leave us confused, but when we take a long look, we see that God causes righteousness to prevail. The psalmist declares, "I believe that I shall see the goodness of the Lord in the land of the living!" And then he adds, "Wait for the Lord; be strong, and let your heart take courage" (27:13–14 RSV).

God's Mercy

In defense of God's fairness, let us not forget His tender mercy. The truth is that we do not want God only to be fair. We do not want mere justice. His mercy is our only hope.

Put two sheets of paper before you. On one write everything you have done that was perfectly good, with no touch of evil in it. Then on the other sheet write everything you can remember doing that has been wrong in any way. Think not only of your deeds; think also of your words and even your thoughts. Study your own lists, and they will lead you to fall on your knees, praying, "God, be merciful to me a sinner!"

In a certain town there was a man—call him Mr. X—so righteously stiff that his own children were deprived of many of the simple pleasures they had a right to enjoy. One Sunday afternoon some boys were playing ball out behind a grove of trees. Someone came by and asked, "Boys, why don't you go around to the other side of the trees where you will have more room?"

One of the boys spoke up: "Mr. X would see us there, and we don't want him to see us playing ball on Sunday." "But God sees you here, doesn't He?" "Sure," said the boy, "but we'd a lot rather God see us than Mr. X."

Those boys had a better understanding of the nature of God than did Mr. X. God is not a self-centered, pious hypocrite. He is a loving Father. Listen to these words: "But when he was yet a great way off, his father saw him, and had compassion, and ran, and fell on his neck, and kissed him" (Luke 15:20). Those words describe a father's action toward his son who was coming home. Jesus said that God is like that!

Look at Jesus

Finally, and most important, when deciding whether God is fair, look at Jesus. He was born nearly two thousand years ago, was crucified at about the age of thirty-three, and was buried. In three days He was up and living again, visiting and talking with His friends for a few weeks. Then He left them, and no one has seen His physical body since.

Since that happened, men have sought to understand the true meaning of it all. Great numbers have believed that Jesus was God—that the great God who made the earth came and walked on it for a time, and in doing so left a true picture of Himself.

The record of Jesus' life on earth is the only real proof of God's love and compassion. You cannot find such a picture of God in nature. True, there are beautiful flowers, majestic mountain peaks, and gentle rains from heaven. But there are also fierce storms, the withering heat of the sun, and the dread disease of cancer.

But we can understand this God who came to earth "to seek and to save the lost." He came on a mission, and to accomplish it He gave Himself as a ransom for the sins and shortcomings of mankind. The cross will forever stand as our supreme evidence of a loving, suffering, forgiving God.

Someone said, "I had a thousand questions to ask God—until I met Him." You will continue to wonder why this or that happened the way it did. But as you come to know God, you will come to have faith in Him, and you will gladly trust your life in His hands. Then, nothing can destroy your peace.

3

DIVIDENDS FROM TROUBLES

Recently I was on a plane, going to Arkansas to give a series of sermons. Flying used to make me nervous but now I have worked out a little procedure that enables me to relax. Just before we take off, I pray this little prayer: "Lord, bless the pilot and the crew; bless the airplane; and if there is an accident, may it not be fatal. In Christ's name. Amen." Then I leave the plane in the hands of the pilots and the Lord.

Actually I have flown so much now that I take it for granted that everything will be all right. However, on this particular trip I did get a bit nervous. Instead of landing when we reached the airport, the big plane began to circle. It kept circling for forty minutes or more, and I knew there was something wrong but didn't know what it was. Down below I saw two fire trucks and an ambulance drive out and park at the runway where we were to land.

I was on a tight schedule to make my appointment, and at first I was wondering if I might miss my connection. As we continued to circle I forgot about getting where I wanted to go—I just wanted to get down! I was like the mouse who said, "I don't want any cheese—I just want to get out of the trap." I never did learn what the trouble was. We did land without mishap and everything turned out well.

Thinking of that experience, I thought that life is somewhat like that. We are going along happily and contentedly—and then something goes wrong. The man who met me at the airport in Arkansas is a farmer. He owns several thousand acres of that rich Mississippi Delta land. As we drove along, he told me about his experience the year before. In July he had the finest crop he had ever seen. He felt sure it would be his best year. Then it started raining and it kept raining. As a result, he lost heavily.

A lot of men have had business setbacks that came unexpectedly and were not their fault, but they suffered because of them. All of us have experienced disappointments of one kind or another; no person can live long without some kind of suffering. But God never promised a life with no trials, nor did He promise skies that would always be sunny.

Faith in God is not an insurance policy against physical pain; neither does it insure us against mental pain that results from such things as fear, anxiety, loneliness; neither does our faith protect us in every case from the remorse and agony over some sin of the past, though it may be repented of and now forgiven; and neither does faith protect us from the hurts and bruises that sometimes result from the environment in which we live.

As someone said:

> God hath not promised:
> Sun without rain—

Joy without sorrow—
Peace without pain.

But God does promise His companionship, strength, and love. "Lo, I am with you always" (Matt. 28:20), said Jesus, not only to His first disciples but to each one of us.

I get a lot of mail from people who are sick. I suppose the sudden loss of physical health is one of the greatest losses one can experience. One lovely morning in May some fifteen years ago, I started to drive to northern Georgia to preach. It was a beautiful day, and I looked forward to being in the mountains again. Instead of the mountains, however, I ended up in a hospital room. For a time I wondered if I would ever preach anywhere again. Since that experience, I have had a more sympathetic heart toward those whose bodies have been struck down by illness of any kind.

Since, sooner or later, every one of us is likely to experience physical illness to some degree, let me say some things about it. The time of sickness is not the time to solve all our problems. Sickness throws us off balance emotionally; to some extent, one loses his sense of poise and equilibrium. Little things become big things when one is not feeling well.

In one place where I lived, my study was at the church in a room off the sanctuary. Often I found it necessary to work late at night. Usually a church sanctuary is a delightful and inspiring place; when it is filled with people, with lights and music, it is a joy to our hearts. But late at night, when it is dark and empty, a church can be a gloomy place. A big empty building will creak and groan. In the daytime you pay no attention, but when you're alone at night, those noises become bothersome. A few times that church had been broken into by thieves, and when I was there alone, a noise would make me wonder if some sinister person were fixing to burst in upon me. I wasn't afraid, but I sometimes found it difficult to concentrate.

In a sense, sickness is like being alone in the darkness: you wonder what might happen; your imagination can get out of hand. A sleepless night, when you are sick, seems like an eternity. You don't think with your normal clarity, and things get out of proportion.

So, in a time of illness, do not let your mind continually focus on your troubles. When things have settled back to normal, there will be time enough to see about certain critical issues.

All through the Bible we are promised dividends from troubles. Trials and tribulations are gold mines from which may be taken some of life's riches prizes. So, to begin with, instead of praying, "Lord *when* am I going to get out of this?" it is better to pray, "Lord, *what* am I going to get out of this?"

The Bible tells us: "We glory in tribulations also: knowing that tribulation worketh patience; And patience, experience; and experience, hope: And hope maketh not ashamed; because the love of God is shed abroad in our hearts" (Rom. 5:3–5). Often it is that tribulations do lead to the flooding of our souls with the bright sunshine of God's love.

Time to Develop Faith

Many have told me of rich rewards they have received from a time of illness, suffering, and enforced inactivity. It is a time to think. John Greenleaf Whittier wrote:

Drop Thy still dews of quietness,
Till all our strivings cease;
Take from our souls the strain and stress,
And let our ordered lives confess
The beauty of Thy peace.

In a time of quietness we have a chance to rest, an opportunity to evaluate life more properly, to develop a sympathy for other people. We learn that the whole world can keep going without us, and that gives us a wholesome sense of humility. When we are sick we gain some other values, such as a greater appreciation of God's gift of health, and a realization of the higher purposes of life; we lose some of our selfish independence and develop an appreciation of and dependence upon others; we become aware of and thankful for the achievements of medicine and science. Most important of all, sickness can become a time when we develop a stronger faith and become surer of God.

Once there was a woman who was trying to turn on the light in a telephone booth. A passerby said, "Lady, if you will shut the door, the light will come on." In a sickroom we can shut the door to the outside world for a time. We are not required to carry on all our daily responsibilities, and in shutting the door, we often experience the light of the Lord coming on.

St. Paul wonderfully wrote, "I am persuaded, that neither death, nor life, nor angels, nor principalities, nor powers, nor things present, nor things to come, nor height, nor depth, nor any other creature, shall be able to separate us from the love of God, which is in Christ Jesus our Lord" (Rom. 8:38–39). That is his way of saying that no matter what may come, you can still hold on to God and you need never step outside the circle of His love.

In a time of illness and trouble we worry about the things we might lose—especially about losing our chance to live in this life—but nothing, not even death, can take away from us our most precious possession—the warm, comforting, sustaining love of God. This assurance takes from us the strain and undue worry; it gives to us a sense of security and well-being.

George Matheson beautifully wrote:

> There is an Eye that never sleeps,
>   Beneath the wind of night.
> There is an Ear that never shuts,
>   When sink the beams of light.
> There is an Arm that never tires,
>   When human strength gives way.
> There is a Love that never fails,
>   When earthly loves decay.

In a time of illness—a time of helplessness and near despair—we can lean back easier on that "arm that never tires" and we find it sufficient. During a war, someone noted a sign in front of a church in London that said, "If your knees are shaking, kneel on them."

One other thought—as we kneel we find the strength to hold on. Emerson said that a man is a hero not because he is braver than anyone else but because he is braver for ten minutes longer. Put your hand in His hand, and God will give you the help to keep you brave as long as necessary.

4

WE CAN GET THE FORGIVENESS FEELING

In the Lord's Prayer we pray, "Forgive us our debts," (Matt. 6:12). Instead of saying "debts," many use the word "transgressions," or "sins," but the word "debt" has vivid meaning for most of us. Debt can be a terrible burden; to know that all your debts are paid in full is a glorious experience.

As I went through college, I had to borrow some money to help pay the expenses; so when I started preaching, I was in debt. I was required to make a payment each month on what I owed. I had an old car, but it finally wore out completely and I traded it in for a new one. I signed a contract to pay so much a month until it was paid for. Paying for that car is where I got my best idea of eternity.

I remember some of the letters the finance company wrote when I got behind on my car payments. They were fearful! Once, when I got two months behind, a man came after the car. I never talked so fast in my life! If I could preach as well as I talked to that man, I would make a lot of converts.

In those years we didn't have to have many clothes, but we had to buy some along the way. It was illegal to go without clothes. But what we bought was always on the installment plan. I remember an overcoat I bought for $5 down and $5 a month. I missed so many payments that by the time I finally made the last one, the coat was worn threadbare. We even bought our groceries on credit. My limited credit at the grocery store is one reason why I am so skinny today.

In those years it took every dollar I got to pay for something I had already eaten up or worn out. It worried me to be in debt. I don't remember asking God to let those debts be "forgiven," but I did pray many times asking God to show me how to make enough money to pay up everything.

We worked hard, the Lord helped us, and finally there came a day when all our debts were paid. There were no more mean letters about our payments being behind, and what money we had was clear and free. A great burden was lifted from my mind, and I felt new joy and happiness.

But debts for cars and clothes and other things are not the worst ones. How about the burden of debt that comes because of our sins against God? How can we ever feel that debt is paid?

Most of us know the burden of being in debt. I used to trade with a grocerman who kept his accounts in a big book. I would pay him as I could and he would mark "paid" by certain items, but the trouble was that I had to keep on eating, so I would charge other things. It was hard to get that page completely paid off.

As children we got the idea that God kept a list of our sins in a big book. Each of those sins was like a debt we owed and would have to pay. Some of our sins we felt we could pay by doing something really good. Sometimes, when trouble or misfortune came, we felt God was making us pay in that way. We never could catch up because we would do other things that were bad and they would be recorded against us.

Finally we come to the place where we feel we can never pay off our debt of sin to God. We feel hopelessly doomed. Then we remember that Jesus taught us to pray, "Forgive us our debts." Will God answer that prayer? Can we know that our page in God's book is marked "Paid in Full"? Can we really feel forgiven? We can if we will accept six facts—not only in our minds, but also in our hearts:

1. God wants to forgive us; He loves us and understands us. The Bible tells us, "If we confess our sins, he is faithful and just to forgive us our sins" (1 John 1:9). Why confess? God already knows all about us. Confession is our recognition that what we have done is wrong; it also means our desire to have it taken out of our lives and hearts. We do not need to persuade God to forgive. As we look at the cross we realize that He loves us and goes to the uttermost for us.

2. Forgiveness means that we are again on good terms with God. It does not take away the memory of our wrongs; the pain and sorrow of our failures will always remain with us. Neither does forgiveness take away all the consequences of our sins; some of our sins we will pay for until we die. But forgiveness does mean that a

right relationship with God is restored. We can again respond to His love. His power and peace can flow freely into our hearts. We do not feel cut off and alone. We feel in our hearts that He is our Father and we are His children.

3. God does not expect us to rid ourselves of our sins. The old song has it right: "Just as I am, . . . I come, I come!" God is not some tyrant who takes delight in making us feel condemned and who wants to whip us. I once had a schoolteacher who seemed to get real joy out of using a big leather strap. I was so afraid of him I never learned much in his class. God is not like that. He says, "I know what is troubling you. I don't expect you to conquer all the evil thoughts and desires in your heart. But come and let Me help you, and together we will find the right way. I will walk with you to guide and strengthen and help you find joy and satisfaction."

4. When forgiven, we can go on. God expects that. He doesn't want us to keep on confessing the same sin. He doesn't want us to keep chewing over the past. When Jesus says that God is a Father, that helps me because I had an earthly father who was like what I want to believe God is. One of Papa's rules with his children was to settle whatever wrong we had done before we went to bed. If needed talking to, he never put it off until tomorrow. After the matter was settled he never mentioned it again, nor would he permit us to.

God is a Father who settles things. Forgiveness means that we have been set free to go on living, and God expects us to go on. Face it, settle it, go on—that is the way to deal with sin before God.

5. Forgiveness means that we surrender a wrong and we surrender to God. Why do we do something that is

wrong? Because we can't help it? No, because we don't want to help it. We do wrong things because we enjoy them, or because we profit by them. As long as the joy we receive from wrong is greater than the joy of a right relationship with God, we shall keep on. But when we decide, truly decide, that we want God more than that wrong, then we are willing to give it up.

Also, we cannot say to God, "I am Yours, but on my terms." Again and again have I talked with someone in regard to making his life right with God. Often one has replied, "But I am not sure about what God wants me to do." My reply is, "Completely decide that you will do the right thing. Then, when you have committed yourself, God will show you what the right thing is." God gives insight to those who trust Him.

6. If we do not feel forgiven, it is likely because of our own pride. It is so easy to tell ourselves, "I'm not such a bad fellow. I really don't need any help." We think of many good things we have done. We list the better qualities of our lives. Then we remind ourselves of the mean things other people do that we haven't done. We decide we can get along without God's forgiveness. But such talk is only pretending; we know that we are guilty and that we cannot save ourselves. It takes a strong man to get on his knees before God.

In *Pilgrim's Progress*, we recall how Christian was making his way toward the Eternal City. On His back was the burden of his sins. He came to Calvary, climbed to the top, and knelt at the cross. The sins were loosed, rolled down the hill into a sepulcher, and were buried forever. Then Christian said with a merry heart, "He has given me rest by His sorrow and life by His death."

Forgiveness is a miracle that God performs. I do not explain it. I simply say,

> In my hand no price I bring;
> Simply to Thy Cross I cling.

5

UNANSWERED PRAYERS

Prayer is the subject of more letters that come to me than any other subject. Many people write requests for prayer, many ask how they should pray in regard to a particular situation, many ask why they have not had an answer to some specific prayer. Often someone writes, "The Bible says, 'Ask, and it shall be given you.' I have asked, but it has not been given me."

Many whose prayers are not answered are bitter and resentful. They wonder if God plays favorites and hears only certain ones. Many are confused and frustrated. They have prayed, and now they do not know which way to turn.

In reply, I want to say, first, that God does hear and answer prayer. In "The Cotter's Saturday Night," Robert Burns said, "They never sought in vain that sought the Lord aright!" Underscore that word *aright*—that is the key. The Bible tells us, "Ye ask, and receive not, because ye ask amiss" (James 4:3). As I read the Bible I find listed many causes of unanswered prayer. Look at some of the more common ones.

"And ye returned and wept before the Lord; but the Lord would not hearken to your voice, nor give ear unto you" (Deut. 1:45). Through His servant Joshua, God had told the people what to do; they paid no attention and did as they pleased. God's later refusal to hear their prayers was the result of their disobedience. One condition of prayer is our willingness to obey God in our lives.

Jeremiah 29:13 tells us: "And ye shall seek me, and find me, when ye shall search for me with all your heart." Halfheartedness is another cause of unanswered prayer. If we are not entirely dedicated to our own prayers, we should not expect God to waste time with us.

The Bible tells me, "If I regard iniquity in my heart, the Lord will not hear me" (Ps. 66:18). That does not mean that one must be perfect in order to pray. Surely even the vilest can pray. It does mean that we must "abhor" evil, that the desire of our hearts is to live right.

"But let him ask in faith, nothing wavering. . . . A double minded man is unstable in all his ways" (James 1:6–8). Stability is required of one who would pray. Our minds and hearts must have a fixed purpose, and we must hold steadfastly to that purpose.

By far, the main reason for unanswered prayers is that our prayers are not within the will of God. Our Lord was careful to add to His prayer, "Nevertheless not my will, but thine, be done" (Luke 22:42). We do not have full understanding, and even though one is completely sincere, from God's view it may be clearly seen that his prayer is not best. Our faith must be such that we trust Him with the answer. Let us ever be mindful that our larger prayer is that we be fully surrendered to God's will.

Three Essentials for Prayer

It has been beautifully said, "Between the humble and contrite heart and the majesty of heaven there are no barriers; the only password is prayer." It bothers me that so few people seem to use that "password" and thereby deny themselves so many of the blessings of heaven that are available to them.

A "humble and contrite heart" is the first essential. One of the finest verses in the Bible is 2 Chronicles 7:14: "If my people, which are called by my name, shall humble themselves, and pray." Notice that we are not told to pray for humility; we are told to humble ourselves. It is such a temptation to become proud, to feel self-sufficient, to recognize no need for God. Sometimes we must be put on our backs before we ever look up.

Too many of us are like the Pharisee in the temple who prayed, "I thank thee, that I am not as other men are" (Luke 18:11). We compare ourselves with someone who has failed along the way, and we take secret pride in another's downfall. That is the reason we are so attracted to gossip—it makes us look so good in comparison! Not enough of us are like the publican who prayed, "God be merciful to me a sinner" (Luke 18:13).

Not only must one be humble in order to pray; he must also have faith. There is probably no passage in the Bible that I read more often than Mark 11:22–26; that is the passage that describes how faith can remove mountains, and in which Jesus said, "I say unto you,

What things soever ye desire, when ye pray, believe that ye receive them, and ye shall have them."

Believing is a process of mental picturing. So often, instead of picturing the answer we want, we continue to look at the troubles we have. We concentrate on our fears instead of our faith, our problems instead of our powers, our sins instead of our Savior.

In that same passage, after He had talked about faith and believing, Jesus said something else: "And when ye stand praying, forgive, if ye have ought against any." A wrong spirit toward another person, hate, hurt feelings, envy, jealousy, can block our prayers completely out.

Humility and faith are two essentials of effective prayer. The third essential you will find in John 15:7: "If ye abide in me, and my words abide in you, ye shall ask what ye will, and it shall be done unto you." *Abide*—that is the key word. Sometimes the answer comes immediately, sometimes the answer tarries—but we must continue close to Christ, developing our love for Him, allowing His love to fill our own lives more completely, meditating day and night upon His words.

Jesus said, "Men ought always to pray, and not to faint" (Luke 18:1). "To faint" means "to give up, to quit." Many times we miss the answer because we stop praying too soon. *Humility, faith, abide*—those are the three key words to answered prayer.

A-C-T-S-S

It is easy to get into a spiritual rut and reach the place where we go through the motions without receiving the power. Especially is this true in our praying. It is a temptation to say the same words every time we pray without really thinking and without putting our hearts into what we are saying. I am constantly seeking to develop new spiritual techniques.

Recently I have hit upon a word that I like to keep in mind when I pray. The word is ACTSS ("acts" with an extra *s*). It is an appropriate word for prayer because all prayer should result in acts. I needed that extra *s* because I use the word as an outline for prayer.

A is for adoration. Surely all prayer should begin with our thinking of the Lord. The most wonderful collection of prayers is the Psalms. Sometime read some of the Psalms, noting how much is given to praise of God: "O Lord our Lord, how excellent is thy name in all the earth!" (8:1); "I will sing unto the Lord, because he hath dealt bountifully with me" (13:6).

Kahlil Gibran, in *The Prophet,* says, "You pray in your distress and in your need; would that you might pray also in the fullness of your joy and in the days of abundance." All real prayer begins in adoration of God.

C is for confession. As one feels the presence of God, as one thinks of His purity and righteousness, he naturally feels even as Isaiah felt. When Isaiah saw the Lord high and lifted up, he fell on his face, saying, "I am undone; because I am a man of unclean lips" (6:5). We read, "If we confess our sins, he is faithful and just to forgive us our sins, and to cleanse us from all unrighteousness" (1 John 1:9). That is a wonderful promise.

T is for thanksgiving. One of my favorite songs is, "Count your many blessings, name them one by one." Many people never think of God except when they want something. Like any father, God is glad when His children come asking, but don't you suppose He also wants us to talk with Him sometimes about so much that He has already given?

S is for supplication; that is, prayer for others. In 1 Samuel 12:23 we read, "God forbid that I should sin against the Lord in ceasing to pray for you." Notice the wording in the Lord's Prayer: the pronouns "our" and "us" predominate. Never forget—praying for another person makes a difference to that person.

The last *S* is for submission. "Not my will, but thine, be done" (Luke 22:42). Prayer is not a means by which I seek to control God; it is a means of putting myself in a position where God can control me. Instead of my prayer being "Give me," it must become "Make me."

6

THE FIRST LAW
OF FAITH

Rabbi Louis Binstock told about a man who had all the financial resources he needed, community standing, and every reasonable hope for happiness. He appeared to have everything, yet he came to the rabbi to say that he had "nothing for which to live."

The man was desperate. When the rabbi said, "You are in the House of God. . . . Give yourself over to the grace of His peace," the man's eyes flashed with bitterness. "The same old-time bunk. . . . Have faith in the Lord—and presto! all your troubles are over and life is beautiful forever afterwards." The man was not interested in that. He got up and reached for his hat.

The rabbi seized his arm and pulled him back. There was an "I-won't-find-help-here" look in the man's eyes, and the rabbi talked slowly: "You are going to help yourself. You have access to a great storehouse of dynamic power, but you have not been using it. That storehouse is faith."

The man's mouth curled with contempt: "If I possessed such a storehouse of faith, would I come to you? Sure, I need faith. But how do I get it? Where can I find it?" He was not the last man who has asked those questions about faith: Where can I find it? How do I get it?

In answer, the rabbi told him an old Chinese tale about a little fish who once overheard one fisherman say to another, "Have you ever stopped to think how essential water is to life? Without water our earth would dry up. Every living thing would die." The fish became panic-stricken. "I must find some water at once! If not, in a few days I will be dead!" And the fish went swimming away as fast as he could. But where could he find water? He had never heard of it before.

He asked the other fish in the lake, but they didn't know. He swam out into the large river, but no fish there could tell him where to find water. He kept swimming until he reached the deepest place in the ocean. There he found an old and wise fish. He gasped, "Where can I find water?" The old fish chuckled. "Water? Why you are in it right now. You were in it back home in your own lake. You have never been out of it since the day you were born." The little fish began the long swim back home, saying, "I had water all the time, and I didn't know it."

So it is with faith. You don't find faith. You don't get faith. You simply use faith that you already have. When a baby is born, God gives it faith just the same as He gives it hands and feet. A child needs to learn to walk, but it is born with the capacity to walk. The teacher cannot give a child intelligence; the teacher teaches the child to use its intelligence. The child cannot be given music; the teacher teaches the child to express the music it possesses.

As energy cannot be created or destroyed, neither can faith be. But faith can lie unused within us. It can be covered up and not used.

We Bury Faith under Fears

We were born "bundles of faith." Nothing is more trusting than a child; but instead of developing that faith, we usually concentrate on teaching the child fear. We make sure the child learns that knives will cut, cats will scratch, dogs will bite, fire will burn, automobiles will run over him, water will drown him, disobedience will bring a whipping, and ugly words will result in a mouth-washing with soap.

Downtown one day I actually heard a mother say to her little boy, "If you don't hush crying, I'll let that mean policeman yonder put you in the dark jail!" What a wonderful way to smother a child's faith with unreasonable fear.

As we grow older we learn other fears. A schoolboy can fail an examination; a bigger boy can teach a little boy how much a lick of the fist can hurt; a teenager can be socially slighted. We can learn the meaning of privation; we experience the disappointments of love, the pain of a broken heart, the disillusionment of the treachery of a friend, the shock of business failure, the burden of a sense of guilt.

It's no wonder that many people who have so emphasized their fears have had their faith buried and forgotten. A scientific magazine some time ago declared that all normal children possess qualities of genius. When you think of your own precious little one as a genius, you are entirely correct. The article claimed that mediocrity doesn't occur until later life. All children are geniuses, but hardly any adults. What happens? No one loses his mental power, but our power becomes buried.

Study closely the dealings of Christ with people and you will see that this was the basic principle by which He worked. He changed people by releasing them. There was Matthew who had let greed make him a slick traitor to his own people. Jesus did not condemn him; He held before Matthew the vision of the highest. Like a magnet drawing a piece of steel, the vision of his possibilities drew out Matthew's real self and made him Saint Matthew. Jesus used His power to make people believe in themselves, and that worked the miracle of change.

There is a heartwarming play called *Seventh Heaven*. It opens with the return of Chicot, the battle-blinded French soldier. He has come back to his sweetheart, who had starved and suffered in a dismal attic room, but she had never faltered in the conviction that her Chicot would return. In her joy of being with him again, she cries that she now can live in her "seventh heaven." He replies, "If you believe it, it's so—if you believe it, it's so."

Faith is not believing something that isn't so. Jesus taught that if we believe something, it will become so. He said, "What things soever ye desire, when ye pray, believe that ye receive them, and ye shall have them" (Mark 11:24).

We All Live by Faith

How can I get faith? Where can I find it? You don't get faith—you already have it. The only place you can find it is within yourself. And the only way you can find it is to look for your faith instead of your fears and your failures.

People die, businesses fail, automobiles are wrecked, jobs are lost, homes are broken up, friends are betrayed, lives are ruined. When you fill your mind with that sort of thing, no wonder you lose sight of your faith and think you have lost it. But just for one day, keep a list of the times you express faith. You will be surprised.

I step out of bed in the morning onto the floor. I believe the floor will hold me up. I take a drink of water. The water comes from a muddy river contaminated with filth. In many places in the world a person would not dare drink water until it was boiled. But I drink the water believing it has been purified. I eat scrambled eggs for breakfast. My wife could have put arsenic in the eggs, but I have faith that she didn't.

I stop at the filling station for ten gallons of gasoline. I don't have a can to measure the gas—I have faith that I'll get what I pay for. I stop at the mailbox to mail a payment on my life insurance. I am depending on that insurance to mean a lot to my wife and children if I should die, to help me if I should get sick, to be a friend to me if I should be unable to work when I am old. That insurance means a lot to me, yet I mail the payments to an office I have never seen, to be handled by people I will never know. I have faith that they will do what they say. Space doesn't permit the naming of the many times I use faith in one day.

Along with sixty-eight other people, I got on an airplane one day. As we were waiting for the plane to take off, I got to figuring how much sixty-eight people weighed. Allowing 150 pounds per person, the total was more than 10,000 pounds. Their baggage added another 2,000 pounds. Then I got to figuring the weight of the plane. It must have been as much as 50,000 pounds—maybe twice that much. Then I began thinking—in a few moments we would be going down that runway at 150 miles per hour. Beyond the end of the runway I could see tall trees and big rocks on the ground. If we went into those trees and rocks we would all be killed. But I looked at the big motors on the plane, and I believed they had the power to lift that big plane above the trees. Looking at only the weight, I was fearful. Looking at the motors, I had faith.

So it is in life. We automatically use faith in a thousand different ways, but sometimes when we come to a place where we must consciously use faith, we shrink back. Instead of thinking of your loads to lift, think of your own abilities, the support of other people, and especially the help of God. And as you think of your power instead of your problems, you will find that faith comes easily and naturally. And you will not then be afraid of failure.

You already have faith—that is the first law of faith.

7

TWO MORE LAWS OF FAITH

Every person has faith. Also, every person has fears. In life the difference is whether you start with your faith or with your fears. Some people think first of the difficulties when facing an undertaking; other people think of the possibilities.

There was a lady who had a stroke of paralysis that left her leg severely crippled. She had great difficulty learning to walk again. In fact, she surrendered to a wheelchair. Her doctor was a very wise man and he refused to let her stay in that chair. One day he told her to stand up; then he told her to walk. Slowly she put forward that crippled left leg, but she sank back in the chair unable to complete the step.

However, the doctor told her to stand up again. Then he told her to take the first step with her right leg, the one that was not paralyzed. She did that, and she found that she could walk. The wise doctor then told her to remember that she could walk if she would always put her best foot forward. This is one of the essentials of faith. Start with your faith, and your paralyzing fears will not be able to hold you back.

One of my closest minister-friends is an example of this principle. When he was six years old, his older brother accidentally shot him. The bullet went through his right hand and his left arm. Several of his fingers were shot away and his left elbow was forever ruined. But that accident did not hurt his spirit. In fact, his crippled hand and arm caused him to develop his faith more completely.

He got through high school but then had no money for college. So he got an old typewriter, learned to type, and paid his expenses through college by working as a part-time secretary. He wanted a Ph.D. degree, so he went to Yale. For his doctor's dissertation, he chose a study of ninth-century manuscripts written in Vulgate Latin. He didn't know Vulgate Latin, but he learned it. Also, in order to complete his research, he had to learn six other languages: Greek, Hebrew, German, French, Aramaic, and Syriac. To pay his expenses, my friend worked in the cafeteria and at night he read proof in a newspaper office from eleven o'clock until four o'clock in the morning. He got his Ph.D. degree and also made an important contribution to biblical knowledge.

I have conducted two revivals in his church and stayed in his home during those weeks. We would talk until late at night, and he greatly inspired me by his great courage and optimism. I said to him one night, "You might have held up your crippled hand and your undeveloped arm and given up in defeat."

He replied, "We all have limitations of some kind, and we all have abilities. I thought about what I could do and never worried about anything else." He then said, "Our limitations can be either stepping stones or stopping places."

Start with Your Powers—Not Your Problems

Whenever I get discouraged, there is no chapter in the Bible that lifts me up and gets me going again better than the fourth chapter of Philippians. I think of St. Paul, who wrote those words. He was a man severely handicapped in body. After he became a man, he never had a home of his own or a loved one who belonged to him.

I think of how he was beaten with sticks and rocks, thrown into jails, and how his frail body must have shivered from the cold. Many times he was hungry. He had a task of preaching Christ to the world, yet against him was the most powerful and ruthless government the world had ever known. In that fourth chapter I think we find revealed the secrets of his great power and unconquerable will.

He writes, "Rejoice in the Lord always: and again I say, Rejoice" (Phil. 4:4). That is, no matter what happens, don't get down in the mouth. Think of God instead of your troubles and express your joy. One of the strongest allies of faith is a smile on our faces.

Also he writes, "Whatsoever things are true, . . . honest, . . . just, . . . pure, . . . lovely, . . . of good report; . . . think on these things" (v. 8). We all have infirmities of some kind. There is something that hurts and holds you back, but instead of concentrating on your troubles, lift your mind to things that will lift you.

In that same chapter Paul says, "I have learned, in whatsoever state I am, therewith to be content" (v. 11). Instead of rebelling against the circumstances of his life, he had learned that in any situation there are opportunities.

Then he gives the secret of his amazing strength, the reason he is never defeated. He declares, "I can do all things through Christ which strengtheneth me" (v. 13). It makes a tremendous difference when you are not totally dependent on yourself.

Also St. Paul gives the reason for his quiet confidence: "My God shall supply all your need" (v. 19). With that assurance, one finds it easy to approach life with faith instead of fear. Every person has limitations and every person has assets. The difference in people lies in whether they start with their problems or with their powers, whether they first step forward with faith or with fear.

The other night I was reading one of Jack London's books. I thought about him. He was nineteen years old before he ever got a chance to go to high school. He died when he was forty years old. Yet he published fifty-one thrilling books.

Lord Byron and Sir Walter Scott each had a club foot and were forced to limp their ways through life. John Milton, Homer, and John Bunyan, three of the greatest writers of all time, were totally blind. When F. W. Woolworth got his first job in a store, his employers would not let him wait on the customers because they said he was too stupid. But men like these will live forever because they emphasized their assets instead of their weaknesses.

Hold On to Your Faith

Someone has pointed out that we live in two worlds— the world that is and the world we want it to be. Faith takes hold of the world that is and makes it what we want it to be. Faith takes the possible and makes it real. It was the great William James who said, "As the essence of courage is to stake one's life on a possibility, so the essence of faith is to believe that the possibility exists." And believing that a better tomorrow is possible, we do have the courage to give our best to the creating of that tomorrow.

The first three laws of faith are these: (1) know that you have faith; (2) start with your faith instead of your fears; (3) no matter what happens, hold on to your faith.

People in Vienna delight in swimming in the Danube River. One of their favorite sports is going up to one of the higher levels of the great river and swimming down toward the center of the city. But every year a few of the swimmers are caught in the whirlpools and drowned.

An expert swimmer says that all such drownings could easily be avoided. He says that water, if given a chance, will always push human beings toward the surface. But one must trust the water. When caught in a whirlpool, many swimmers become panic-stricken and are drowned. However, all one has to do is hold his breath for a few moments, and the water will thrust him clear and he can easily swim to safety.

So it is in the stream of life. We have the faith to start off on some high adventure. We are happy in our hopes and confidently we move forward. Then we become caught in some whirlpool of life, and instead of making progress, we are violently thrown around. Our strokes lose their natural rhythm. We become panic-stricken; we press harder or surrender to failure. But if we hold on to our faith, it will never fail us.

One of the grandest men of our time, or of any time, was Winston Churchill. But back in 1915 he was demoted from an important position and branded as a failure. For twenty-five years he was lost in political obscurity. But though he was lost from the public eye, he never lost his faith. In 1940 the stream of life pushed him to the surface again, and he was ready to write one of England's most glorious chapters.

In this connection we quickly think of Columbus. He had faith in a great idea. But his friends deserted him, his wife died, and he was even forced to beg for bread. He waited and worked for seven long years before he got enough help to begin his journey across the sea.

For sixty-seven days he sailed. Storms ravaged his ships, his men threatened mutiny, but Columbus stayed with his faith. It was as Joaquin Miller wrote:

> What shall we do when hope is gone?
> Sail on! Sail on! Sail on! and on!

And Columbus discovered a new world.

Don't give up your faith. There is a new world ahead for you, too.

8

ANOTHER AND ANOTHER OF FAITH'S LAWS

Now, I want to set down one of the supreme principles of faith. It is: Don't be afraid to trust your heart. I got it from a young couple who had come to talk with me about their plans for marriage. It seemed that it would be very difficult for this marriage to succeed, and I discussed with them some of the obstacles in their path to happiness together.

There were considerable differences in their backgrounds, both financially and socially. They were of different religious faiths, and I pointed out how each could be hurt in the years to come. There were some other problems. I really hoped they would decide to take more time and possibly reconsider.

Finally the girl spoke up. I had much admiration for her because of the circumstances under which I had come to know her. Once I had been on an airplane that ran into a rather heavy storm. In the turbulent air, the plane was pushed around considerably. Some of the passengers got sick, and the rest of us got mighty scared. This girl was the stewardess on that plane, and she moved among the passengers with a calmness and courage that was wonderful to see. Now, feeling the threat of some stormy weather that might lie ahead in her flight into matrimony, she was no less calm, and her answer was wonderful. She said, "We love each other, and we are not afraid to trust our hearts."

Recently I was preaching in another city, and after the service this couple came up to speak to me. I had not seen them since their marriage, and I had wondered how it was with them. She said, "You need never worry about us. We have risen above the storms and we have clear sailing."

It was Pascal who said, "The heart has reasons which reason does not know." Not only in marriage, but in most of life's high ventures, in order to have faith you must learn to trust your heart. Faith is never unreasonable, yet there are times when feeling is stronger than reason, and we must sometimes trust those deep inner impulses.

Dr. Norman Peale tells of one morning when he was in a Sunday school class. Along with the other boys, he was listening to the teacher tell about the courage and faith of Christ as He turned His face toward Jerusalem. It meant meeting His enemies head-on. It meant a cross. But He did not hesitate. The teacher said, "I wonder if any boy in this class is willing to follow Him."

Twelve-year-old Norman Peale felt something happen in his heart in that moment, something that reason could never explain. From then on, that feeling in his heart became the guiding force in his life. It led him into the ministry—and what a glorious ministry his has been! But the Dr. Peale the world knows today would never have been if he had been afraid to trust his heart.

One of the most moving scenes in the life of our Lord occurred one morning after breakfast. The trials and the cross were now behind Him, and He was soon to go back to the Father's house. But what about the future of His work on earth? He had come to build a church, to establish a kingdom, to bring all mankind into brotherhood, peace, and righteousness.

Was it all an impossible dream? Would His coming result in failure and defeat? It depended, I think, on one man—Simon Peter. Simon did not have the education, culture, and mental ability of some of the other disciples, but he was a natural leader of men. The direction Simon took would be the direction they would all take.

It was now only a few days before the Lord's ascension. During breakfast that morning, He must have been thinking of how Simon had denied Him during the trials; how, when courage was called for, Simon had played the part of the coward. After breakfast Jesus slipped over by Simon's side. He might have embarrassed His disciple before the others, but He did not even mention his shameful failure. Instead He said, "Simon, . . . lovest thou me?" (John 21:15). He did not argue with Simon; He simply wanted to know what was in his heart. And Jesus was not afraid to trust a man's heart.

In truth, Jesus always knew that if He could capture a man's heart, He would have the man; so His method of winning people was through the heart. We recall how a rich young ruler came to Him, and the Bible says, "Jesus beholding him loved him" (Mark 10:21). If the young man had returned that love, his life would have been forever different. Maybe he did love Jesus but was afraid to trust his heart.

Faith is never blind. Faith is never unreasonable. But there are times when the only guide we have to our rendezvous with destiny is the faith in our hearts.

Certainly Jesus was not afraid to trust His heart. His method of winning men is through loving men. As little children we learn to sing:

> Jesus loves me, this I know,
> For the Bible tells me so.

And in old age we sing:

> Jesus, Lover of my soul,
> Let me to Thy bosom fly.

You do not doubt His love for you, yet it often seems unreasonable. We are such a mixture of good and bad that we are ashamed of ourselves. An old British soldier wrote these words:

> My padre, he says I'm a sinner,
> John Bull, he says I'm a saint,
> But they are both of them bound to be liars,
> For I'm neither of them—I ain't.
> For I'm a man, and a man is a mixture
> Right down from his very birth.
> Part of him comes from heaven
> And part of him comes from earth.

Jesus knows that, but He still loves us; and because He trusts His heart, He never loses faith in us. We too must learn to trust our hearts.

Maintain a Spirit of Humility

If one wishes to possess and keep a calm, confident faith as he goes through life, it is absolutely essential for one to maintain a spirit of humility. Faith and humility go together, and without one the other quickly dies.

Out of Catholic tradition comes this wonderful story. There was a rumor that a girl in a convent was performing almost unbelievable miracles. The pope sent St. Philip of Neri to investigate. After a long journey, he finally reached the convent and asked to see the girl. As she entered the room, he pulled off his muddy boots and asked her to clean them. Haughtily she drew up her shoulders and scornfully turned away. St. Philip left and when he got back to the pope, he said, "His Holiness must give no credence to the rumors. Where there is no humility, there can be no miracles."

Maybe St. Philip was thinking of the time when the Lord of Lords poured water in a basin, got on His knees, and began to wash the disciples' feet. And how He spoke to them that night of the temptations to come within the next days. And how Simon Peter loudly boasted that though everybody else might deny the Lord, He could depend on Simon to hold steady and firm. And how after that supper they went out into the garden and Jesus got on His knees to pray to God, but those disciples felt no need of prayer; they were sufficient unto themselves. Certainly it is true—where there is no humility, there are no miracles.

There is a story of a young college girl who visited the home of Beethoven. She asked permission to play on the great master's piano. She played a few bars and then said to the guard, "I suppose all the great artists have played this piano during their visits here?" He replied, "No, Paderewski was here two years ago and someone asked him to play. But he declined, saying he was not worthy to touch that piano." All great people are humble. That is why they are great.

The pattern is set forth in 2 Chronicles 7:14: "If my people, which are called by my name, shall humble themselves, and pray, and seek my face, and turn from their wicked ways." Notice, we are never taught in the Bible to ask for humility; we are to humble ourselves. Every Sunday night I invite people to come and kneel at the altar. Occasionally I am asked if one cannot pray as well sitting in the pews. My answer is, "I can't." I think there is much value in the act of kneeling. In itself, it is a humbling experience.

And when one is humble, he does not feel self-sufficient. Then it is easier to pray, to seek God, and turn away from wrong. The remainder of that verse tells us what God will do after our humility, prayer, true seeking of Him, and forsaking of wrong: "Then will I hear from heaven, and will forgive their sin, and will heal their land"; that is, God will hear, forgive, and bring peace and prosperity. When we meet the conditions and the promise of God is fulfilled, we are afraid of nothing and we face the future with serene confidence.

9

THREE BASIC PRINCIPLES OF LIVING

What is going to happen in the future? A lot of people are wondering, and a lot of people are afraid. I find many who are haunted by discouragement and despair; they see nothing good ahead. Many people see no reason for living. But one does not have to be the victim of tomorrow. I am one who believes a man can take a firm hold on his future and be the master of it.

The Bible says, "And now abideth faith, hope, charity" (1 Cor. 13:13). In that sentence you find the three basic principles of determining your own future. "Faith, hope and charity"—let those words sink into your mind and become part of you. They will lead you into a life that is successful in the very highest and best sense.

Faith

Learn to have faith. The first cause of failure is lack of faith. Failure and faith are incompatible words—they simply cannot exist together. If you have faith, you will not fail; if you fail, it is a sign that you do not have faith. Faith may have setbacks, but faith never knows failure.

The famous football coach Knute Rockne had four rules for the selection of the boys on his great Notre Dame teams. He said: (1) I will not have a boy with a swelled head, for you cannot teach him anything; (2) I will not have a griper, kicker, or complainer; (3) I will allow no dissipation; (4) I will not have a boy with an inferiority complex—he must believe he can accomplish things.

Read again number 4 of Rockne's rules; it is the most important. The psychologist William James, who probably understood people better than any American who has ever lived, confirmed Mr. Rockne's rule. He said, "Our belief at the beginning of a doubtful undertaking is the one thing [note that he said—the *ONE* thing] that assures the successful outcome of our ventures."

But faith is not something that suddenly comes to a person in some magical manner; it is something that must be learned. The best guide I know for learning faith is contained in these words from the Bible: "Jesus said unto him, If thou canst believe, all things are possible to him that believeth. And straightway the father of the child cried out, and said with tears, Lord, I believe" (Mark 9:23–24).

The first step is to get the word "impossible" out of our vocabulary. We begin losing faith by saying, "It can't be done," or something similar. We begin learning faith by believing it can be done.

Here is a little plan that works wonders: keep count of the times in one day when you say or think something is impossible; at the end of the day write that number down. The next day concentrate on reducing the times you allow yourself to think in a negative fashion. See how many times you reduced the number of the previous day. Continue day by day to reduce your use of "impossible," and gradually more and more areas of your life will move into the realm of the possible. You will develop new courage and strength as faith begins to grow within you. Try it and you will see.

But that is not the full answer. Notice, the man replied, "Lord, I believe." Merely to say "I believe" tremendously increases one's power, but to begin with "Lord" is far greater. In fact, true faith must begin with God. We recall that Jesus said, "The things which are impossible with men are possible with God" (Luke 18:27).

The longer I live, the less confidence I have in myself, but the more confidence I have in God. I am conscious of my own weaknesses and limitations, but I have become increasingly conscious of God's strength and power. And as I shift my confidence from myself to God, I find my faith becoming stronger. Somehow—I don't always see how, but I know that somehow—God will always know what to do and will have the power to do it. That gives me faith.

Hope

"Faith, hope, charity"—I have spoken of the power of faith; now, let us consider hope. One of the finest pieces of literature is Tennyson's "In Memoriam." In it we find these words: "The mighty hopes that make us men." Truly, hope is one of the ingredients it takes to make a man.

You may be familiar with G. F. Watt's picture entitled "Hope." It portrays a poor woman against the world. Her eyes are bandaged so that she cannot see. In her hands is a harp, but all the strings are broken save one. These broken strings represent her shattered expectations, her bitter disappointments. That one last unbroken string is the string of hope. She strikes that string and a glorious melody floats out over her world. It fills her dark skies with stars. The artist painted a great truth—even when all else is gone, you still can have hope, and no one is defeated until hope is gone.

Dr. Samuel Johnson, the brilliant English man of letters, said that to have a bright, hopeful outlook on life is worth a thousand pounds a year; that is, when one thinks with hope, he will attain far more. Certainly there is much evidence to cause one to believe that the attitude of one's mind determines what happens to him. Job said, "The thing which I greatly feared is come upon me" (3:25). Many are able to say, "That which I hoped has come to pass."

I have a friend who has a deep aversion to hearing anyone use profanity. In his pocket he carries a supply of little cards that he hands out to those he thinks need them. On the card are printed these words: "The use of *profanity* is the sublime effort of the ignorant, uncouth, simpleminded, godless man to express himself—'Thou shalt not take the name of the Lord thy God in vain; for the Lord will not hold him guiltless that taketh his name in vain' (Exod. 20:7)."

I am in hearty sympathy with my friend's campaign against profanity. It is one of man's worst and most useless habits. But, as I frequently point out, the worst profanity is not the swear words people often use. The most profane word is "hopeless." The Bible says, "Hope thou in God" (Ps. 42:5). To become hopeless is to deny God.

Hope is not a dreamy, unreal thing; it is based on the most real thing there is—the existence of the almighty, eternal God. The psalmist said, "Why art thou cast down, O my soul? and why art thou disquieted in me? hope thou in God: for I shall yet praise him for the help of his countenance"; that is to say, when you are disheartened, put God in the center of your thoughts. By concentrating on your troubles, you despair; by concentrating on God, you hope. If you will do that, the day will come when you will have reason to praise God.

It has been well said, "Life is full of glad surprises for those who hope."

Charity

"Faith, hope, charity"—take that word "charity." Wrapped up in it is so much—love, unselfishness, good will, kindness. No person can live unto himself. The reactions of other people in so many ways determine what our own lives will turn out to be. And charity toward others is always the best way to follow.

One of my favorite stories is tucked away in the Book of Genesis. Joseph had been sold into slavery by his jealous brothers. Later Joseph became the king's chief assistant down in Egypt, and due to the famine in their land, his brothers went to Egypt to beg for food. They did not recognize their brother Joseph, but he told them to bring with them their brother Benjamin the next time they came.

This grieved their father Jacob. Since he had lost Joseph, young Benjamin had become dear to his heart. Fearful that Benjamin might be kept in Egypt, Jacob had his sons carry gifts for the Egyptians—balm, spices, myrrh, nuts, fruits, and a double amount of money. And the old man also said, "Take a little honey." Honey represents something sweet and gentle.

To make the most of life, we need to take along ability, training, initiative, faith, and hope—and don't forget to "take a little honey." A kinder, sweeter spirit always wins in the long run.

You remember the old story about how the sun and the wind got into an argument over which was the stronger. The wind said to the sun, "I am stronger. All you do is shine, but I blow, and believe me, when I blow everybody knows it."

They saw a man walking down the road. They agreed to test their strengths by seeing which could make the man take off his coat. The wind went to work but the harder it blew, the closer the man pulled his coat around him. Then came the sun's turn to try. It made no noise; it just quietly began to send warm rays toward the man and pretty soon the man had his coat off.

That is a silly little story, but it illustrates a great truth. Simple, warm, loving kindness works wonders. The Bible tells us, "And be ye kind one to another, tenderhearted, forgiving one another, even as God for Christ's sake hath forgiven you" (Eph. 4:32). Isn't it true that kindness will accomplish so much more than the pugnacious, hard-boiled attitude? Then wouldn't it be a good idea for us to start practicing it a little more?

Robert Louis Stevenson said a wonderful thing: "Anyone can carry his burden, however heavy, until nightfall. Anyone can do his work, however hard, for one day. Anyone can live sweetly, patiently, lovingly, purely, till the sun goes down. And this is all life really means."

WHEN LIFE SEEMS TOO CROWDED

Every so often I get up in the morning saying, "I just cannot do all the things I feel I must do today." Sometimes, in such a mood, I feel confused and don't know where to begin. Then it is I go through a series of three steps that I have found to be of great help. Perhaps others will find these steps helpful.

Make a List

First, I take pencil and paper and make a list of the things I need to do this day. Then I arrange the list in the order I want to take up each task, estimating how much time each will take. Often I find I can do everything on my list and even have an hour or two to spare. Sometimes I find there is too much, so I strike off some of the items that can be put off.

After making my list of things to do, I stop thinking of everything on the list except the first item. When that is finished, I take up the second item, etc. It is amazing how much easier it works out and how much calmer and clearer the mind is when following this procedure. There is an old proverb that says, "The longest journey begins with a single step." Instead of thinking of the long journey, think of the next step.

Once there was an old man who was building a log house, and someone asked if that were not a big job for him alone. He said, "If I had to think of cutting down all the trees, skinning their bark, setting each log in place, and all the other work, it would be a big job. But right now, all I am concerned about is this one log I am working on."

Someone has well said:

> God broke the years to hours and days,
>   That hour by hour and day by day,
> Just going on a little way,
>   We might be able all along
> To keep our spirit poised and strong.

By taking one step at a time, one can walk a long way in a day. And by giving oneself to one task at a time, one can accomplish more than he ever thought he could. If you are a housewife, you cannot wash the dishes, sweep the floor, and make the beds all at the same time. Just put your mind on one task and do that, and then turn to the next. If you are an executive, you can make one decision at a time, refusing to consider the next decision until the first one is settled. If you are a secretary, you can type only one letter at a time.

We squander our power when we try to do one job and carry the load of another job on our minds at the same time. In the Bible we read, "As thy days, so shall thy strength be" (Deut. 33:25); that means that you will have the strength to do what each day calls for. The heavier the days, the stronger you will be.

One Day at a Time

Next, just as you must concentrate on the one task at hand, also concentrate on the living of this one day. Too often we add to this day the burdens of yesterday and tomorrow. It is so easy, and so disintegrating, to review and regret old decisions. Suppose you did make some mistake yesterday? Good! You have learned not to repeat that again. Profit by your mistakes, but stop worrying about them.

Take the two most important decisions of your life, next to your decision for Christ: (1) your choice of a life's work and (2) the decision to marry the person you did marry. Have you wondered if you might not have gone further and been happier if you had taken another road, or married another person? Add to those two questions a multitude of other wonderings about whether you did the right thing, and very quickly life becomes a very heavy burden, indeed.

There is another thought to consider. Not having traveled the road you did not take, you do not know how it would have been. You can easily imagine that the other road might have been smoother, leading more directly to the land of your heart's desire, but that is mere supposition. It likely was not as good as the one you chose.

Anyway, in most cases it is too late to go back and start over again.

Also remember that you have not completed the journey on the road you did choose. You may now be having a difficult time, but it may not always be so. Who knows but that not too far ahead the happiness you are seeking will be on the very road you did choose. So just stay with the journey you are now on, giving your best to this today. Futile regrets over yesterday and appreciation over tomorrow will get you nowhere.

St. Paul learned the secret—"This one thing I do, forgetting those things which are behind" (Phil. 3:13). The Revised Standard Version of the Bible makes Jesus' words clearer: "Therefore do not be anxious about tomorrow, for tomorrow will be anxious for itself. Let the day's own trouble be sufficient for the day" (Matt. 6:34).

There you have it—tackle one job at a time and live one day at a time.

You Are Stronger Than You Think

Now comes the third and final step in my plan: always remember that you are stronger than you think. I doubt if any person ever used all his strength. God made the human body in such a way that there are certain glands that secrete and supply energy when it is needed for an emergency.

I know of a farmer who was sitting on his porch one day watching his son drive toward the house in a pickup truck. Something went wrong and the truck ran into a ditch and turned over, pinning the boy underneath. The father ran to the place, lifted the truck, and pulled the boy out from under it. Later he tried to lift that truck again, but he could not budge it. The emergency had brought forth strength to meet it.

Every mother understands this. One night she goes to bed so tired that she feels she could not walk across the room one more time if her life depended on it. But one of the children becomes suddenly ill and cries out. Immediately the mother is on her feet, ready to watch over and minister to that child throughout the remainder of the night. She had strength she had not known before.

Perhaps this is what the Bible meant when it said, "As thy days, so shall thy strength be" (Deut. 33:25). The Twenty-third Psalm tells us, "Thou preparest a table before me in the presence of mine enemies" (v. 5); that is, in the midst of need God supplies the resources.

Not only did God make our bodies with reserve strength, but also He made our spirits with reserve strength. Sometimes we feel, "I cannot go through this," but when the time comes we find that we can. We can stand far more than we realize. Not long ago I saw listed the title of a minister-friend's sermon; it was: "You Are Braver Than You Think"—and you are. The chances are that when the time comes, you are more likely to stand up with courage than you are to become a coward.

Not only do you have reserve strengths that rise to your aid when the need comes, but more important is the power of Almighty God. Someone asked D. L. Moody if he had "dying grace." He answered, "No, I have living grace, but when the time comes that I need it, God will then give me 'dying grace.'" And we recall how St. Paul prayed again and again that the "thorn in his flesh" be removed; instead, God gave him the "grace to bear it." God supplies the added strength that you need, if you ask Him for it and have faith.

11

MAKING A HARD DECISION

There is an old story about a man who was hired out by a farmer. His job the first day was cutting wood. He worked hard. The second day the farmer put the man out in the field to dig weeds. The sun was hot, but the man threw himself vigorously into the work. The third day it was raining, so the farmer had the man sort potatoes in the barn. It was easy work; all he had to do was look at each potato and put the rotten ones in one pile and the good ones in another pile. At noon the man told the farmer he was quitting. The farmer was amazed. He said, "The first day you worked hard cutting wood, the second day you dug weeds. Now I give you a nice easy job and you quit. Why?" The man replied, "I didn't mind the work, but when I started sorting potatoes, I couldn't stand to make those decisions."

As we go along through life, we don't mind the work; but the hardest part of living is making decisions. That is where most of our failures are—not that we make bad decisions, but rather that we often are unable to decide at all. We remember how Elijah said to the people, "How long halt ye between two opinions? if the Lord be God, follow him: but if Baal, then follow him." Now comes one of the saddest lines in the Bible: "And the people answered him not a word" (1 Kings 18:21). They wouldn't say yes, they wouldn't say no. They just wouldn't say.

We remember the classic story of the donkey standing between two haystacks. The hay was fragrant and the donkey was hungry. Yet he could never decide which stack to turn to. When he was minded to feast off one, the delightful aroma of the other tantalized him. And so it went until, according to the story, the poor donkey stood between the two haystacks and finally starved to death.

That represents a lot of people—people who have never learned to make up their minds. The greatest enemy to life is indecision. When facing some hard decision, take a good look at Pilate. He was faced with the most important decision of all time: "What shall I do then with Jesus?" (Matt. 27:22). We all have that decision to make. We have other decisions, too, and it will help us to see Pilate's problems and the mistakes he made in arriving at his decision.

Pilate was the Roman governor of Judea. Early one morning, a mob brought Jesus before him to be tried. Pilate really had no interest in the case; yet he was young and ambitious, and he wanted to take no chances on his own future. He already had had trouble with the people, and exciting them further might have endangered his position. On the other hand, he had a conscience and a sense of justice. No matter what his decision might be, it would likely cause trouble. So, when faced with a hard decision, Pilate lost out on the greatest chance of his life because he didn't know how to make up his mind.

I have often wondered what the last two thousand years might have been if only Pilate had had the courage of his convictions. Without his permission, Jesus could not have been crucified. Instead of dying at the age of thirty-three, He might have lived to be seventy-three or even eighty-three. Suppose the Lord had lived for forty or fifty more years on this earth? What a difference it might have made!

And Pilate really did not want to see Him crucified. Pilate's was probably the friendliest face Jesus saw at all His trials. "I find in him no fault at all," Pilate said (John 18:38), but he was "on the spot." To release Him would have offended the people, maybe getting Pilate in trouble with Rome and thwarting his personal ambitions. It would have been the popular thing to let Him be crucified.

On the other hand, there was something mysterious about Christ that troubled Pilate. During the trial that morning, a message came from Claudia, Pilate's wife, saying, "Have thou nothing to do with that just man: for I have suffered many things this day in a dream because of him" (Matt. 27:19).

It is possible that Claudia had come to know Jesus. Maybe one day, as she passed through the city, she had seen Him lifting some crippled man off his bed; maybe she had paused as He was speaking and listened to His wonderful words; maybe their eyes had met as they chanced to pass on the street; maybe one of their servants had told her about Jesus. Someone has well said:

> I did but see him passing by,
> And yet I'll love him till I die.

Maybe Claudia was interceding for Him, or maybe she had had a dream and was frightened at what might happen, and Pilate shared that fright. Certainly he did not want to make the decision concerning Jesus.

I find it in my heart to condemn Pilate, but before I do, I must point out that we too have important decisions to make. And in condemning Pilate, we condemn ourselves. Instead of facing up to his responsibility, Pilate began to run from his decision.

Evasion

First he tried to evade a decision. He said, "Take ye him, and judge him" (John 18:31); that is, put the responsibility on the crowd. We do that many times when faced with some decision of life. Instead of determining our own course, we say, "Everybody else is doing it. I'll follow the crowd." But that never satisfies, and it didn't work in Pilate's case. Pilate sent Jesus to Herod (Luke 23:7); he tried to put the decision on somebody else. But Herod sent Him back. We can never evade our own responsibility. I have had many people come to me for counseling on problems, but one thing I have learned: you cannot make someone else's decision for him. Pilate made one more effort at evasion: he tried to substitute Barabbas. Instead of squarely facing the issue, we bring up some other issue and evade the main one.

Compromise

When faced with a hard decision, we often seek to compromise with it if we cannot evade it. When Pilate faced the question, "What then shall I do with Jesus?" he did not want to crucify Him; yet it would have caused trouble if he had let Him go. So Pilate took a middle course. He wouldn't say yes and wouldn't say no.

The Bible says, "Then Pilate therefore took Jesus, and scourged him" (John 19:1). Then said Pilate, "Behold the man!" (v. 5). He was saying, "Hasn't His suffering now been enough?" But the crowd was not satisfied. Nobody is ever satisfied with compromise. They shouted, "Crucify him" (v. 6). Now Pilate had lost his chance. James Russell Lowell was right when he said:

> Once to every man and nation comes the moment to decide, . . .
> And the choice goes by forever 'twixt the darkness and the light.

Decisions have a way of not waiting, and if we evade and compromise, decisions move on out of our reach and we are left behind in defeat. No one has ever put it better than Shakespeare:

> There is a tide in the affairs of men,
> Which, taken at the flood, leads on to fortune;
> Omitted, all the voyage of their life
> Is bound in shallows and in miseries.

Then Pilate dramatically "took water, and washed his hands before the multitude, saying, I am innocent of the blood of this just person: see ye to it" (Matt. 27:24). It would be wonderful if we could evade our hard decisions and then simply wash our hands of them. But such is never the case. We have a responsibility for many things, and we must accept the responsibility of our decisions.

The world has never let Pilate loose from his decision. I am persuaded that God never let him off, either. But also Pilate couldn't let himself off; he had to live with his failure the balance of his days.

I don't know what Pilate's life was after that day, but we may rest assured that he was never a real man again. His failure to decide tore away the inner strengths of his soul and left him a defeated coward. Over Jesus' cross Pilate put the words, "JESUS OF NAZARETH THE KING OF THE JEWS" (John 19:19). The people wanted the sign changed but he stubbornly refused, saying, "What I have written I have written" (v. 22). He might have changed the inscription, but what he said applied to his own life. Opportunities come; we make some decision, saying yes or no, or we run away from the decision. Whatever—

> The Moving Finger writes; and, having writ,
> Moves on. . . .

There is a legend that Pilate, like Judas, found life unbearable. Instead of hanging himself, he tried to run away and eventually got to Switzerland. There he drowned himself in a lake, and the legend is that on moonlit nights one can see the ghost of Pilate, forever moaning, forever washing his hands. Whether the legend is true does not matter. What is true is that the universe offers no place to retreat from the reality of life. No matter what the cost, better for Pilate had he made the right decision. So it is for me—for you.

12

WHAT'S YOUR HURRY?

The minister met me at the plane. He said, "We don't have time to wait for your baggage. Someone else will get it. You are to speak at the club in twenty minutes." As we hurried from the airport into town, he told me the schedule for the week.

Each morning at nine o'clock there was to be a talk on television and at ten o'clock a church service; then each night another service at the church. There were to be three civic club talks, talks at two high schools, and one talk to the women's club. It all added up to nineteen speaking engagements in four and a half days. In addition, certain hours had been announced for personal counseling.

I got along fairly well until Wednesday night. I went to bed that night, but I couldn't get to sleep. I read a magazine, I walked about the room, I took a warm shower, but nothing helped. I have some little mental tricks I sometimes use to get off to sleep, but they all failed. I had let myself get wound up too tightly. Finally I did get a little restless sleep, but the next morning I felt terrible.

After the ten o'clock service, I told the pastor I would be gone for the remainder of the day. I started walking slowly down the street, going no place in particular and in no hurry to get there. A number of people spoke to me and stopped and talked awhile. It reminded me of living in a little town where you can enjoy visiting up and down Main Street.

I walked on past the city limits until I came to the big bridge on the river. I found a comfortable place to sit down, and I sat there for two hours watching the river. I thought of Grove Patterson's experience: while sitting on a bridge watching the water flow, he thought of the expression, "under the bridge," and how the troubles and hardships eventually go "under the bridge."

From the bridge I could see the point where two rivers flowed together. One of the rivers was almost clear, the other extremely muddy. For a short distance after they came together, you could distinguish the water of each, but a little farther on, the clear water took on the brownish color of the other. I thought about how we let evil thoughts come into our minds and how the evil soon colors all our living. I made some mental notes for a sermon about that.

At the end of the bridge was a tiny hamburger place. I had one with onions; in fact, I asked for an extra onion. It tasted real good. I didn't care whether or not it left an odor on my breath. I had been so pious all that week that I was in the mood to do something daring. Eating onions made me feel independent.

I walked on along the road until I came to a cemetery. I remembered a prescription a physician gave a patient: spend an hour a day for a week walking in the cemetery, and remember that the people here thought they had to do everything, but now the world is going along without them.

"Bargitis"

"Bargitis" is one of the worst of our modern diseases. Watch the cars waiting for a red light. At the first flicker of the light changing, many drivers stomp down on the accelerator and "scratch off." If a car ahead hesitates for even a second, they impatiently blow the horn.

I even notice signs of "bargitis" at church. Some people sit on the edge of the pew and never really settle down. If the service runs a minute overtime, they impatiently look at their watches. When the benediction is announced, they rush toward the door. I sometimes want to stand at the door and ask, "What's your hurry?" Most could make no answer. They are really in no hurry; they are just afflicted with "bargitis."

I spent an hour walking among the graves. During that hour I was the only person there. I thought about how quickly someone is forgotten and how others take our places. It is not so important that we carry the world on our shoulders, as we sometimes think.

I got back to the hotel in time for dinner before the preaching service that night. I felt rested and relaxed. When I got back to my room after the service, I went to bed. I picked up my Bible from the table and opened it to the Thirty-seventh Psalm. Next to the Twenty-third, that is my favorite psalm. It was written for people who get disturbed and overwrought.

The Thirty-seventh Psalm is gentle and tender; like a sweet, kindly mother putting her hand upon the brow of a restless child, the Psalm begins, "Fret not thyself." It goes on to say, "Delight thyself also in the Lord; and he shall give thee the desires of thine heart" (v. 4). Further on we read, "Rest in the Lord, and wait patiently for him" (v. 7). All the way through, the psalm leads one to a calm and a triumphant faith. That night I slept easily, and the next day I felt rested and strong.

Many times I have listened to the motors of a giant airliner. As the plane roars down the runway for the takeoff, it takes all its power to lift itself off the ground into the air. But very quickly after takeoff you can tell that the pilot has eased back the throttles; the big plane climbs into the air and finally levels off. Then the big motors are throttled down still more. The pilot will tell you, "If I run the engines at full power for long, it will harm them."

So it is with each of us. There are times when we must go at our full power. But if one does not learn to ease back the throttle, level off, and hit a steady cruising speed, eventually he will become torn asunder by strain and stress. I am not thinking so much of the strain we put on our bodies as that which we put on our minds.

I know a man who is confined to a wheelchair, yet he is burning himself out. His mind is constantly rushing to this and that. He worries about his business; he has an uneasy conscience that tortures him; he is filled with unrest and tension. He has never learned to level off.

The Power of God's Word

I used to give a lot more time to personal counseling than I do now. I have learned that more can be accomplished through a church service that is carefully planned with that purpose I mind than through individual talks.

In a church service the minister has many helps that he does not have when talking with some person—helps such as the sacred building, the music of the organ, the choir and the people singing together, the uplifting and stimulating presence of other people in the congregation. As the minister speaks from the Word of God in that atmosphere, it more deeply penetrates the mind of the person hearing him. The Word of God in the human mind can work miracles.

Why are people so rushed, so restless and ill at ease? Often it is because we have not found satisfaction in life. Maybe we are running away from a sense of failure. The Bible says, "For God hath not given us the spirit of fear; but of power, and of love, and of a sound mind" (2 Tim. 1:7). Not long ago one of the most brilliant and prominent men in my state came to see me. He had been drinking and could hardly walk up the steps. I asked, "Why do you drink as you do?" He said, "I am trying to find a better world in which to live." Not being able to face his world, he tries to escape into another world through liquor.

St. Paul has a better answer for those times when the "spirit of fear" begins to grip you. If you will let God into your life, you will begin to feel a new power. You will not be afraid to face up to life. Also, you will feel love. Your thoughts will become outgoing, and you will be possessed by good will. You will lose your bitterness. As a result of losing that spirit of fear and as we begin to possess power and love, the Bible says, we develop a sound mind; that is, our mind becomes unified. Faith in God pulls life together, gives it high purpose, sure direction, and guidance.

In his book *Stay Alive All Your Life,* Dr. Alston Smith tells of being called at 2:30 in the morning to visit a boy who was dying. When the minister arrived, the physician said he did not believe the boy would live until morning; he was in a coma. The minister found the family gathered around the bedside. He opened his Bible and began to read some of the great passages of faith and inspiration.

As Dr. Smith read, a deathlike stillness reigned in the room. He felt the power of the Scripture's words and continued to read for a full hour. At dawn the physician examined the boy again. He said, "He has passed from coma into rest. The pulse is better. The indications are that he will live." The boy did live. He had been unconscious during that hour of Bible reading, but the power of faith had entered his system through his subconscious mind. It had stimulated his will to live.

Get quiet, then read slowly and thoughtfully the Thirty-seventh Psalm. See how it will deeply affect your own mind.

13

GIVE YOURSELF AWAY

Jesus gave us one of the supreme principles of life when He said, "He that findeth his life shall lose it: and he that loseth his life . . . shall find it." These words are recorded in the tenth chapter of Matthew (v. 39), a chapter every Christian ought to study carefully.

In this chapter are the names of the twelve men Jesus chose to be His disciples, and His instructions to them. He told them of their mission in life and said that they were not to worry about providing for themselves. "Provide neither gold, nor silver, nor brass in your purses," He said (v. 9). He reminded them that they would meet opposition and would be persecuted, but they were not to fear "them which kill the body, but are not able to kill the soul" (v. 28).

Jesus told His disciples that they could afford to trust their safety and security in the hands of their Father. He pointed out how God notes even the fall of one sparrow, and He said, "Fear ye not therefore, ye are of more value than many sparrows" (v. 31). He charged His disciples that the one thing they were to fear was that they might lose their courage and fail to confess their Lord. He said, "Whosoever shall deny me before men, him will I also deny before my Father which is in heaven" (v. 33).

Following Jesus means that He must be put first. He demands that love for Him must take precedence above even the love we have for our own families—our fathers or mothers, our sons or daughters; there can be no rivals to our affection for Him. "He that loveth father or mother more than me is not worthy of me: and he that loveth son or daughter more than me is not worthy of me" (v. 37).

It is very popular today to say that religion can make one successful, happy, confident, and relaxed. But Jesus doesn't appeal to the selfish desires of those who would follow Him. Instead, following Him demands a cross. His words were: "He that taketh not his cross, and followeth after me, is not worthy of me" (v. 38).

There is a little book nearly fifty years old entitled *The Cross in Christian Experience,* written by Dr. W. M. Clow. In that book Dr. Clow distinguishes between a burden, a thorn, and a cross; no one I know has been able to say it better. He says that a burden is the normal load that life lays upon every man—his daily work and responsibilities. A thorn is an affliction that some must bear—it may be a handicap, an illness, a deep sorrow, or one of many things. The cross is a voluntary denial of ourselves in order to carry His load. Burdens and thorns are thrust upon us, but only volunteers carry crosses.

Don't Be a Holdout

Then Jesus comes to the supreme law of discipleship and of life. Give yourself away, He says; don't be a holdout. Be willing to lose yourself and your life for His sake, and He promises that you will find life anew. I heard it said of a young man recently, "He has not found himself." Many people are in that predicament!

Some years ago a tailor phoned to say that a man had bought me a suit. When I went down to get measured and to select the cloth, the tailor said, "The man wants you to have the best," and he showed me the most expensive cloth he had. A couple of weeks later the suit was delivered to me.

It fit me perfectly. It was the finest suit I had ever had. Never have I been prouder of a suit. But it was so nice that I wanted to wear it only on special occasions. When I went away I never took that suit because I thought it might get worn. I didn't want to put it in my bag because it might get wrinkled. In fact, there were very few occasions when I wanted to wear my good suit, and through nearly ten years I kept it.

One day that same tailor was measuring me for another suit. I said, "You remember that first suit you made for me? I still have it." He said, "Why, you can't wear that suit. It is out of style." Not only was it out of style; from hanging in my closet so long, it had actually become badly worn. By holding out, I had lost my good suit. I had saved it to death.

Down in Mississippi I had dinner in the home of an elderly lady. Her children were grown up and gone, her husband had died; now she was alone. During dinner I commented on the lovely tablecloth. After dinner she opened a large chest and carefully lifted out some of most exquisite linens I have ever seen.

She told me that when she was a young lady, her mother had taught her to sew and had helped to make these lovely things. When she married she had her chest filled—I think that is what they call a "hope chest." I asked, "When do you use these lovely things?" Rather sadly she replied, "I never have used them." Now it is too late; the one she made them for is gone. She actually lost her lovely things by saving them.

When I first began preaching, I had difficulty getting up enough to say. I spoke of this to my father, who had been preaching a long time. During our conversation, I told him of a very fine illustration I had read. He said, "Why don't you use that in your sermon next Sunday?" I replied, "I am saving that for a special occasion." Then my father gave me the best lesson I ever received in the art of preaching. He said, "Use everything you have in your next sermon; then you will find something else."

I have a minister-friend who has the finest filing system I have ever seen. But the tragedy is that he has spent so much time saving his material that he has never had time to prepare his sermons. The result is that he has pretty much lost out as a preacher.

Saving is a virtue that may become a fault.

All the Way

One of our favorite hymns has these words:

> Where He leads me, I will follow,
> I'll go with Him, with Him all the way.

86

The truth is, you can't go with Him at all unless you decide to go "all the way." In fact, that principle applies in so many areas of life.

A young man who is near and dear to me recently went to another city to begin a new job. He wanted to make good, and we talked about it. I told him not to worry about how much he was paid or how soon he got a raise. I told him not to worry about his position; if he were told to sweep the floor, he should sweep it the best it has ever been swept. I told him to forget his own pleasures and give himself to his work. I know that if he follows that path, he will find the life he really wants.

When my wife and I got married she had one hundred dollars that she had saved up from her salary as a schoolteacher. She gave it to me to put in the bank with my money. Actually I didn't have any money in the bank, but I hadn't told her because I was afraid she wouldn't marry me if she knew how poor I was. I told her that the money was hers and she should keep it for special things that she might want. She said, "No, I don't want anything that isn't ours." That is really the only way a marriage can work. You must put all you have into it.

We could all be happier and accomplish so much more if we weren't afraid to turn loose and give our best. I got a letter from a lady who said that for some years she had wanted to tithe, but she didn't have the courage. Finally she did take the plunge and started giving a tenth of her income. She told me what a great joy it has brought to her life.

You remember when your children were little. You could stand one on a high place, hold out your arms, and tell him to jump to you. The child would leap forward into space. Of course, you could have jumped back and let the child fall and get hurt. But the child never thought about your doing such a thing. He had faith in you and knew that your arms would catch him and hold him.

Our Lord wants us to have that sort of faith in Him. So before He said, "He that loseth his life for my sake . . ." (Matt. 10:39), He told us that God notes the fall of even one little sparrow. He said, "Fear ye not therefore, ye are of more value than many sparrows" (Matt. 10:31). The psalmist said, "I have been young, and now am old; yet have I not seen the righteous forsaken, nor his seed begging bread" (37:25). Come to think of it, neither have I. Have you ever seen the righteous forsaken?

Where in your life have you been holding out from the Lord? Is there some sin you should let go? Some cross you should lift up? Why not trust Him now and by faith lose your life for His sake. He promises that you will find the very life you have been holding back.

14

GOD'S LOVE AND MAN'S FREEDOM

To reveal some truths about God and man and life, Jesus gave us the story of a man who planted a vineyard. The man took pains to make it complete: he put a hedge around it to protect it, dug a wine press, and even built a tower so that the workers could see any enemies who might approach. Everything possible was done to make the vineyard a good and profitable place to work.

Then the owner put the vineyard into the hands of some tenants and went to another country. At the end of the year he sent his servants to collect the rent. Instead of paying, the tenants beat the servants and even killed one of them. The owner sent other servants, but they received the same treatment. Finally he sent his own son, feeling sure the tenants would respect him. They killed the son, thinking they could thereby possess the vineyard for themselves.

The story ends in judgment: the tenants will have to face the owner and be punished. The vineyard will be given to other tenants. Jesus concluded the story with another parable: "The stone which the builders rejected, the same is become the head of the corner" (Matt. 21: 33–46).

In this simple story some great lessons for life are set before us, which we shall consider.

The Providence of God

The bountiful providence of God comes first. The vineyard represents the world that God made and freely gave to man the privilege of living in. Read again the story of the creation, and you will find that man was the final step in the process. God might have created man earlier and made man help Him in the work of making this world; instead, God finished the work and then made man.

Isn't it wonderful how God took rivers and oceans, mountains and plains, rocks and trees, air and sky, and all the other parts, and put them together in one world? Every need of man has been met. God knew man would be cold in the winter, so He put life in the seed and fertility in the soil. He put electricity in the air to do man's work and light the darkness.

A little boy was in the hospital. His father fixed up a large surprise-box of lovely gifts, one to be opened each day. So has God done for us on earth. Every day man finds new surprises that God has put here. We discover the atom with its marvelous power; it was wonderful to open a package and find the prevention of polio; tomorrow the package we open might be a chemical that will cure or even prevent cancer. Isn't it exciting to think about what man might discover? Isn't it even more exciting to realize there is a God who loves people to the point where He makes such bountiful provision for them?

A hog will eat acorns under a tree day after day, never looking up to see where they came from. Some people are like that—but others are led through their blessings to realize the love of their heavenly Father.

The Freedoms of Man

Next, consider the freedoms of man. "Freedom" is a misused and misunderstood word. Actually, no person is free without limitations; no person is free from obligations. The owner of the vineyard left the tenants to live as free men, yet there were some restrictions. There was a hedge about the vineyard, and they could use only so much land. They were not free to sleep all day; they had responsibilities of work, and also there was rent to pay.

So is man's freedom limited. We were not free to choose the day and generation in which we would be born, our heredity, or even the color of our skin. Some are born with a talent to sing, others with a talent to work with their hands. But we are all free to use our opportunities or let them slip by, to double our talents or bury them in the ground, to work our vineyard or let it grow up in weeds.

I am free to be good or bad, to fill my life with hate or with love, to live for self or to live for service, to make the world better or worse, to count for something or to count for nothing.

Because God loves us, He desires for us our highest good. So God doesn't just let us go and forget us;

He throws around us protecting restrictions. Tagore expressed it wonderfully: "I have on my table a violin string. It is free to move in any direction I like. If I twist one end, it responds; it is free. But it is not free to sing. So I take it and fix it into my violin. I bind it, and, when it is bound, it is free for the first time to sing."

George Matheson wrote:

> Make me a captive, Lord,
> And then I shall be free;
> Force me to render up my sword,
> And I shall conqueror be.
> I sink in life's alarms
> When by myself I stand;
> Imprison me within Thine arms,
> And strong shall be my hand.

Love Restricts Freedom

Because a parent loves his child and desires his highest good, he restricts the child's freedom. The child must study his lessons, eat proper food, go to bed at a reasonable hour. There are many "musts" that should be put into a child's life. Sometimes the child rebels and thinks the parent does not love him, but because love always desires to accomplish good, love can never release the child from obligation and responsibility. Sometimes parental love degenerates into weak sentimentality that demands nothing and accomplishes nothing.

God gave to man the gift of freedom, but God also gave the gift of love, and love restricts freedom. Because we love, we are not free to do some things; because God loves, He is not free to let us do some things. He gave us laws to live by; they restrict some of our freedoms, but they also accomplish our higher good. God wants us to be our best, therefore He seeks to "make us His captives." The good that we develop within ourselves is the rent God wants and expects to collect from us, His tenants.

Love always desires the highest good for the one loved. A mother loves her son, so she wants him to have a healthy body. She will prepare the proper foods and patiently sit at the table coaxing him to eat. If he is sick, she will sit all night by his bedside caring for him. She wants him to be a person of fine character, so she teaches him the principles of life, works to create the right environment for him to live in, and throws around him every possible good influence.

If the child does wrong, she punishes. We smile when we say it, but it is true that punishment hurts her more than it hurts him. No matter what trouble he may get into, or how sorry he may become, his mother never gives up on him. A dear mother past eighty years had told me about the pain she was suffering; her severe arthritis gave her pain every time she moved. In the same conversation she told me of the pain in her heart because of the wrongs of her son. She looked at me and pitifully asked, "Why is God keeping me here?" I sat silently trying to think of an answer. But then she gave her own answer, "He is keeping me here to keep me praying for my boy."

Love Can Be Rejected

God built a wonderful world and put His children here to live. He wants His children to be happy and wholesome, to reach their highest possibilities, to achieve their greatest good. One by one He sent such men as Elijah and Isaiah, Amos and Hosea, Jeremiah and John the Baptist, but the people rejected them.

God might have said, "I gave you clear directions how to live. You disobeyed My commands, you rejected My wisdom, you refused My love. Now you must suffer the hell of a guilty conscience, the consequences of your own stupidity, the prison of your own sins. You have had your dance—now you must pay the fiddler."

God didn't say that. Instead, "For God so loved the world, that he gave his only begotten Son, that whosoever believeth in him should not perish, but have everlasting life" (John 3:16). God did not say, "I could give My Son for your sakes, but no laws of justice would demand that. He would have to go the length of dying on a cross, and I couldn't stand that." He didn't say that because He loves, and love gives its very all.

Why do men reject God's love? We say everybody wants to be loved, but to say that is to misunderstand the meaning of true love. Jesus made the truth plain in the story of the owner of the vineyard who sent his servants and finally his son to collect the rent from the tenants. Instead of paying the rent, the servants killed those who came.

The tenants said, "Come, let us kill him, and let us seize on his inheritance" (Matt. 21:38); that is, instead of accepting our responsibilities, let us serve our own selfish desires. Selfishness is the reason we reject God. We take all that He has given and use it for our own gain, our own vanity, our own comforts.

Let us never forget that the love of God has moral depth and it makes great demands. We sing silly little songs with titles such as "Somebody Up There Likes Me," and we talk about "The Man Upstairs," and we think of God's love as something that fits into a jukebox. But God's love demands high living. When Jesus saw men of great promise giving themselves to fish nets, He said unto them, "Follow me, and I will make you fishers of men" (Matt. 4:19). Love calls to the highest life.

To accept God's love demands that men repent of their sins and turn from their wicked ways. It caused Zacchaeus to make restitution for what he had stolen; it caused Paul to come down from his lofty perch in life and give himself in service; it sent a Schweitzer into Africa. But so many men are tempted to push God out and take over for themselves. We fool ourselves when we think we can take over God's creation.

Bishop Edwin Hughes told of preaching one morning about man's stewardship. He said that everything belonged to God and that man is only a tenant here. That same day he had dinner with a farmer. In the afternoon the farmer showed the preacher his fields and then said, "I have the deed to that land. Does it belong to me?" The preacher wisely said, "Ask me again a hundred years from now."

So Jesus pronounces judgment on those who reject God's love. God's judgment comes not as a result of His anger but because life simply will not work on any basis other than God's way.

Charles L. Wallis points out that some have called the disaster of crumbling buildings following the San Francisco earthquake an act of God, but a distinguished architect, after investigating the tragedy, reported, "Dishonest mortar was responsible for nearly all the earthquake damage in San Francisco." When men build their lives or their society with "dishonest mortar," eventually the judgment will come.

So Jesus said, "The stone which the builders rejected, the same is become the head of the corner" (Matt. 21:42). In those days a cornerstone was used to hold two walls together. It had to be strong and sound. Sometimes the very stone needed was discarded and later the building fell. The builder might then have said, "If I had only used that stone." And those who reject Christ and His way will someday say, "If I had only followed His way, my life would not have ended in this disaster."

15

GET RID OF YOUR SPIRIT OF INFIRMITY

It is pathetic to see so many people stumbling through life half-defeated, unhappy, frustrated, and often bitter and disappointed. Life can be a wonderful experience.

One of the finest stories in the Bible is only three verses long—Luke 13:11–13. There was a woman whose back was so bent she was "bowed together." That is a terrible handicap. Jesus saw her—He always has an eye out for those who need help. The Bible says, "He called her to him." He is the same Christ today as He was then. At this very moment He may be concerned with your need. He may be calling in some way to you.

Remember that St. Luke recorded this story. Luke was a medical doctor. He had treated many people and had become a wise student of human nature. He saw that the woman's trouble was not really her bent back; he reported that she had "a spirit of infirmity." For eighteen years her back had been bent. But the bent back had got into her mind, leaving her with a sense of handicap, inferiority, defeat.

To her Jesus said, "Woman, thou art loosed from thine infirmity." In that instance He did straighten her back, but that was not the important thing. He took the bent back out of her mind and enabled her to face up to life with confidence, whether or not her back was bent. He enabled her to rise above that which was defeating her. She found new joy and peace in life.

Understand and Accept Yourself

That experience can come to any one of us. When something is defeating us, we can gain power over it and find new confidence by doing three things. First, we must be willing to understand and accept ourselves. The great psychologist William James quoted a woman as saying, "The happiest day in my life was the day I admitted the fact that I am not physically beautiful and stopped worrying about it."

All my life I have been underweight. People would talk about how thin I was, and it worried me. I did everything I heard about to gain weight. I worried about getting sick. Then one glad day a sensible physician said to me, "You were born skinny and will be all your life, so stop trying to do anything about it." I accepted his advice and have followed it ever since. I am still skinny, but the fact is out of my mind; it is not a problem to me any longer.

In the play *Green Pastures,* Noah said, "I ain't much, but I'se all I got." When one accepts that fact, life takes on new meaning and power. I think of Evelyn Harrala, who was born without hands or feet. She decided one day that since nothing could be done about her handicaps, she would do all she could in spite of them. She graduated from college with honors, became an accomplished organist, and a valuable member on the staff of a large church.

General William Booth, founder of the Salvation Army and one of the great men of all time, was informed that he was going blind. He said, "I have done what I could for God with two eyes. Now I will do what I can without any eyes."

All of us have handicaps of one sort or another. We can let the handicap get into our minds and defeat us, or we can go on in spite of ourselves and win victories.

You Are Not Alone

There is a second step to gaining assurance. Someone quoted the prayer of a humble old man: "Lord, help me to understand that You are going to let nothing happen that You and I can't handle together." If I thought I had to do by myself the things I have planned for the next twelve months, with only my own strength and resources, I would give up and quit this minute.

One of the reasons people lose confidence and get shaky is that they realize they do not have the abilities and strength to do the things they feel they must do. But I don't depend only on myself; I know that other people will help me. Also, I know the Lord will help me.

The last time I talked with Dr. Norman Vincent Peale, we talked about our wives and what blessings they are. During the worst part of the Depression his church in New York was having difficulty meeting its budget. One day his wife said to him, "Our church ought to take over the full support of another missionary." He did not see how they could add $1,200 to their budget at that time, and that was the amount required. He turned her down.

But some wives—most wives—are hard to turn down. She said, "You might as well go ahead and do it because I am going to pray about it." A few weeks later a man attended that church, made a decision for Christ, and joined. A few mornings later Dr. Peale was opening his mail and there was a letter from that man, enclosing a pledge card and a check for $1,200. Dr. Peale thinks the Lord answered his wife's prayer. I think so, too. What do you think?

Of course, God answers different prayers in different ways, but God always does answer. I was talking with one of the best-known newspaper writers in this country. We were talking about prayer, and he told me that the two things he had prayed hardest for, he had lost. He had fervently asked God to save the life of his baby boy who was sick, but the little fellow died. Later he and his wife had another son, but he was born with the life flickering in him. This man walked the corridors of the hospital praying, but they never got the baby home alive.

Yet he is not bitter; neither did he lose his faith. He told me that often, as he is walking along the street, he feels the need of prayer and stops right where he is and talks to the Lord. And he spoke of several instances when almost miraculous answers to prayer have come. He doesn't ask why he lost those two little boys; he trusts God and he goes on.

I have constantly said to my own children, "When you need help in any way, always let me know." I would be very disappointed if one of them said, "I won't ever need you again. I'll handle everything by myself." I want to take a part in their lives. And our heavenly Father feels that way about each of us.

Get Started Living Your Faith

I have said two things: understand and accept yourself; trust in the help of God and other people. I have one more thing to say: get started living your faith the best you can.

The president of a certain company had a large number of people working under him. He took the view that no one person was indispensable; he could always get another to replace any one of his employees who left his business. But gradually he came to feel that there was one girl in his office who was indispensable. He could not explain why that girl was so important. She had no special qualifications. Others did their work as well as she. But he felt the office simply could not go on without her.

Finally he asked her about her life, and she said, "One day changed my life." She told of hearing a sermon in which the minister had said, "Why not try religion for just one day?" The minister explained that the average life spans about half a million hours. Surely one could afford to use at least twenty-four of those hours in such a noble experiment. The girl decided to try it.

She began that day with a quiet devotional, reading some words from the Bible, and praying. She asked God to give her strength to resist any and every evil thought that day. She started to work that morning, saying over and over, "Just this one day I am going to try religion." Whenever an unkind word almost reached her lips, she turned it back with a short prayer. When any fears came, she prayed again and trusted God. When tempted to be less than her best, immediately she stopped and asked, "What would Jesus do right at this moment if He were in my place?" She kept it up through the day.

That night she had a feeling of happiness and satisfaction she had not known before. So, naturally, she decided to try it a second day, and she did. And that became her philosophy of life—"I'll try religion for just this one day." When she was tempted to be her old self in some situation, she would remember the satisfaction she had felt since trying religion, and she would gain the inspiration to keep trying. As the days went by, it became easier for her, and life became increasingly an experience of joy. Later she wrote: "Imagine what it means never to be afraid of anything. Not to be afraid of insecurity, loss of position, not to be afraid of life or death. Imagine what it means to have no ill will. Imagine what it is to be at peace. I suddenly discovered that everything began to flow toward me rather than away from me. Amazing things happened. Life became good, and everybody seemed to love me. Gradually I began to have a sense of well-being."

That "one day" idea is fine. Why don't you try it? And wouldn't this be a good day for the experiment?

16

OVERCOME
YOUR ANXIETIES

We are a curious people. We have developed the resources of the earth; we have all sorts of mechanical
gadgets to make life easier and more interesting; we
are the best fed, clothed, and housed people of all his-
tory—yet we are insecure victims of anxiety. Someone
calls this "The Century of Fear." Another refers to it as
"The Age of Anxiety."

So many of the novels and plays written today are
about unhappy, fear-ridden people who can't find any
answers to life. We are not surprised at this because
many of these are written by people who themselves
have found no answers to life. Anxiety is a problem, to
some extent, with nearly every person today. It is also a
problem that every age has experienced.

Jesus saw anxiety in people, and He said, "Therefore
do not be anxious about tomorrow" (Matt. 6:34 RSV).
I have studied this matter of anxiety a great deal and
have talked with many anxious people. I think the basic

cause of anxiety is the fear that we will be forced into a situation we cannot handle. We are afraid that some circumstance of life will overwhelm us.

To find an answer for anxiety, let's look at one of the most dramatic sea stories of all time: turn to Exodus 14 and read about the dividing of the Red Sea. For ten generations the children of Israel had been in bondage in a foreign land. Life for them was filled with ceaseless toil, and they were bitterly homesick.

Each night around the hearthstones of their crude cabins, they heard the stories of the faith of their ancestors. They learned of Abraham, they were told about Isaac and Jacob, and about Joseph. They maintained the altars of faith; they continued to believe in God; they never gave up their dreams of their Promised Land. Someday they would be free again.

There was a man by the name of Moses who had ruled over them, had then become one of them, and had then disappeared. Now he was back again demanding freedom for his people. "Let my people go," he demanded of Pharaoh. Moses had strange and wonderful power; even Pharaoh could not stand up to him. The great day finally came when the children of Israel packed their belongings and were on their way toward the land that "flowed with milk and honey."

Freedom was not theirs; actually their anxieties were only beginning. Would they be able to find their way through the wilderness? Would they have enough food to live on? Would the land be as good as they hoped? Was this just a trick of Pharaoh's and would he bring them back to bondage? Curiously, anxiety is not born out of adversity; it comes from blessings that we fear we may lose.

When You Are Blocked

As the children of Israel journeyed toward the realization of their dreams, the possession of their Promised Land, the word came that Pharaoh had changed his mind about letting them go free. With his armies, the hated dictator was now after them. They hurried their pace; they broke camp earlier and marched longer into the night. Maybe they could keep ahead of Pharaoh.

Then came that dreadful day when they came to the sea. There it stretched before them to block their path. They had no boats; they could go no farther; they had no weapons to fight the army behind them. There was no hope either forward or backward. Their only course was helpless surrender.

Now comes one of the grandest scenes in the entire Bible. I am not referring to the dividing of the Red Sea. To see the waters roll back and the dry land appear, providing a pathway to safety, was wonderful, but that was really the anticlimax. Even more wonderful was what happened before. In the midst of their anguished disappointment, Moses stood up. Finally he got their attention. Notice what he said: "Fear ye not, stand still, and see the salvation of the Lord, which He will shew to you today. . . . The Lord shall fight for you and ye shall hold your peace" (vv. 13–14).

What a marvelous faith he had! The Israelites had been so busy and hurried that they had forgotten that God could help them. "Stand still," Moses said. We remember how the psalmist said, "Be still, and know that I am God" (46:10). One of our greatest needs is to learn how to quiet our spirits, to still our minds, and give God a chance with us.

As we realize God's presence, the anxieties of life lose their hold upon us. Someone has written:

> Have you come to the Red Sea place in your life,
> Where in spite of all you can do
> There is no way out, there is no way back,
> There is no other way but through?
> Then wait on the Lord with a trust serene,
> Till the night of your fear is gone.
> He will send the winds, He will heap the floods,
> When He says to your soul "Go on."
>
> And His hand will lead you through, clear through.
> Ere the watery walls roll down,
> No wave can touch you, no foe can smite,
> No mightiest sea can drown.
> The tossing billows may rear their crests,
> Their foam at your feet may break,
> But over their bed you shall walk dry shod,
> In the path that your Lord shall make.
>
> In the morning watch, 'neath the lifted clouds,
> You shall see but the Lord alone,
> When He leads you forth from the place of the sea,
> To a land that you have not known.
> And your fears shall pass as your foes shall pass.
> You shall be no more afraid.
> You shall sing His praise in a better place,
> In a place that His hand hath made.

Quiet Your Mind

In a very difficult moment, when it seemed that all was lost, Moses said to his people a word that we also need to hear: "Stand still, and see the salvation of the Lord." In times of anxious fear, our greatest need is to quiet our minds.

In a church of which I was formerly pastor, there was placed a series of twenty-three stained-glass windows depicting the life of our Lord. These windows were created by one of the oldest stained-glass companies in the world. For more than three hundred years this company has studied ways to create windows that will develop a mood of worship in the minds of the people.

The climactic scene of these windows is the one behind the pulpit, directly before the people during the service; it shows the ascension of Christ. More than half of the window is deep-blue sky. Some have said there was too much blue in it, but the artist knew what he was doing when he made it that way.

I was reading recently of a psychologist who had made a careful investigation of the effect of color on the human spirit. After a long series of experiments, he had learned that the color blue reduces tension, blood pressure, heart action, and relieves anxiety. Blue creates an atmosphere in which one can more easily throw off the worries of daily life and let the Spirit of God into his mind.

A friend of mine tells about talking with the man who repairs the windows in the Cathedral of Chartres in France. This man said that the one color which has not disintegrated under the elements during the centuries is the blue used by the ancient craftsmen. He declared that one reason Chartres is so stimulating to the human spirit is because of the deep blues through which the light filters.

The main point is this: If the color through which we look at the light influences our minds and spirits, how much greater are we influenced by the windows through which we look at life. Moses said, "Stand still, and see the salvation of the Lord." That is, first get God in your mind and then look at your problems through the window of your faith. Color your thinking with God, and your anxieties will cease to dominate you.

Jesus did not say, "Do not be anxious about tomorrow"; He said, "Therefore do not be anxious about tomorrow." The word "therefore" makes all the difference! Jesus had just been talking about God's care for the birds and for all His creation. With a God like our God, *therefore* we need not be anxious.

Be still right now for one minute. Let your body relax. Think of God as being right at your side; think of His power flowing into you. Think of Him opening the way through some problem of your life. Feel deep peace possessing your mind. "The Lord shall fight for you and yet shall hold your peace." *Amen.*

17

ALWAYS REMEMBER TO THANK THE LORD

God's chosen people were in bondage in Egypt. He wanted His people to be free, to live in the land He had promised them. But they needed a leader, and God waited thirty generations until there arose a man capable of the task. That man was Moses.

As Moses led the people toward the land God had promised them, he sought to make them people who would be worthy to possess that land and with whom God would be pleased. And Moses could look beyond these people; through him, God was laying the foundations upon which society would be built. Moses gave to the people their moral and ethical standards—we call them the Ten Commandments.

Also, Moses commanded the people to be grateful to God and to express their thanksgiving. One of the spiritual peaks of the Bible is the eighth chapter of the

Book of Deuteronomy; especially during the Thanksgiving season, it would be good for every American to read it. Moses told the people of God's mercies toward them, and he said, "When thou hast eaten and art full, then shalt thou bless the Lord thy God for the good land which he hath given thee. Beware that thou forget not the Lord" (vv. 10–11).

Personally I get a great thrill out of this country that God has given us. Surely it is a "good land." I like to travel around this country. Not long ago I was in Florida to give some sermons; it is beautiful there. Recently I stood in one of the great oil fields of Texas. During the summer I conducted a meeting on the shores of one of the Great Lakes. This year I preached in Kansas, and from my hotel window I could see miles of golden wheat waving on the plains. When I was in New England I saw some of the homes of our early settlers. A little while before that I stood on the shores of the blue Pacific. Before I die, I would like to visit each one of our states.

What a blessing it is to live in our land! We have a billion acres of farmland; five hundred million acres of forest; a hundred million acres of coal, iron, copper, and other minerals; another hundred million acres of land developed into cities and towns. On our land we have 320,000 oil wells, six-and-a-half million farms, thirty-seven million buildings, two million miles of highways.

We have only 6 percent of the world's land area and only 7 percent of the world's population, yet we have 66 percent of the world's wealth, 80 percent of its automobiles, half of its telephones, and more than half of its insurance policies.

Suppose you had been given the privilege of deciding where you would be born? Would you have chosen to be born one of the starving multitudes of India, or perhaps China? Or would you have chosen to be born under the power of a Russian dictator, or in the darkness of Africa? Aren't you glad God let you be born in this land? That is reason for thanksgiving.

Keep Alive the Fire

Once a girl in college sat down with five other girls at a cafeteria table and bowed her head to say grace silently. Some of the girls laughed. When she finished her prayer, she asked why they had laughed. She said, "Aren't you thankful?" One of the girls said, "For what? We paid for the food."

"Where did you get the money?" she asked. "From our families," one replied. "Where did they get it?" was the next question. "They worked for it," was the answer. "Where did they get the strength—where does it all come from?" she asked. That evening, at supper, two more girls said grace before their meal; the next day all six of them said it.

As one thinks of the blessing of this land that we enjoy, surely he is moved to, as one man put it, "an attitude of gratitude." Not only is ours a land rich in natural resources but in human resources as well. During the Thanksgiving season we especially think of those hearty Pilgrims who came to this country on the Mayflower. Half their colony died during that first hard winter, yet in the spring when their little ship left to go back to England for supplies, not a single one of them gave up the struggle and went back with it. It was these people who established our Thanksgiving Day.

One thinks of the kind of people God put here to establish this land—men who could and did write a Declaration of Independence, a Constitution, and a Bill of Rights. Study those foundation stones of our society and you will see that they contain such principles as a firm reliance on Divine Providence and a belief that we are all created free and equal. This is a land of opportunity—for that we are thankful.

William L. Stidger told a story of a rugged mountaineer in Tennessee. Some years ago the government was building a lake there to generate electrical power, and many homes had to be moved. But one man refused to move out of his home. The government officials argued with the man and even built him another home that was not far away and was much nicer. Still he refused to move. They kept asking him why he would not move. Finally he explained that his grandfather had started a fire on the hearth in the old cabin and had instructed his son to keep the fire going as a sacred family symbol. His father had kept the fire going, and before he died, he had transmitted the heritage to his son. The man said, "I must keep alive the fires of my fathers."

So the engineers carefully gathered up the fire from the old hearth and carried it, still burning, to the new home. Then the man was satisfied to move.

That is a good thanksgiving story. It reminds us of both our blessings and our responsibilities. It is important to pause to add fuel to the ancient fires and to ask ourselves from whence came this wonderful land of ours. All that we have comes from the bounty of the Divine Providence.

Carry a Rope with You

I like the phrase "an attitude of gratitude." Actually there are many people who have the opposite attitude. We Americans overcriticize ourselves. Many people read the newspapers every morning just to see how bad things are and to get fresh ideas for criticism.

I remember that when I started college, people were criticizing Herbert Hoover and the Republicans. It wasn't long until we voted out the Republicans and voted in the Democrats; then we criticized the Democrats. Twenty years later we voted in another Republican, and then another Democrat, and all the while we kept criticizing. Recently I heard a man saying that he was supporting Ben Hogan for president. I asked why, and he replied, "If we must have a golfer, then let's have a good one!"

We criticize the farm program, the foreign policy, the Department of Defense. I have even heard some people criticizing the Supreme Court. Listen to people talk and it is the rarest thing if you hear anyone saying good things about the greatest form of government this world has ever known. Actually, we are making ourselves sick through our attitude of criticism.

A. J. Cronin, a wonderful physician and one whose writings have blessed mankind, says, "Nothing brightens life—our own and others'—so much as the spirit of thanksgiving."

Dr. Cronin tells about a doctor in Wales who prescribed for certain types of emotionally disturbed people what he called his "thank-you cure." When a patient came to him discouraged, pessimistic, and full of his own troubles, but without symptoms of a serious ailment, the doctor would give this advice: "For six weeks I want you to say 'Thank you' whenever anyone does you a favor; and to show you mean it, emphasize the words with a smile."

"But no one ever does me a favor, doctor," a patient sometimes complained.

Whereupon, borrowing from Scripture, the wise old doctor would reply, "Seek and you will find."

More often than not, the patient would return six weeks later with quite a new outlook, freed of his sense of grievance against life, and convinced that people had suddenly become more kindly and friendly.

If we would begin each day with the opening words of the One Hundred and Seventh Psalm, "O give thanks unto the Lord, for he is good: for his mercy endureth for ever," it would not only change our own hearts, it would also change our world around us. We would find life to be a new and an altogether worthwhile experience.

An "attitude of gratitude" does more than say, "Thanks"; it changes our way of life. Once a man's car stalled on a lonely road. Another man came along in his car, stopped, took out a rope, and pulled the other car to a garage. He refused any payment but said, "If you really want to show your gratitude, buy a rope and always carry it in your car."

Wouldn't any one of us be happier if we had this attitude of gratitude? So many favors would be done for us, and we would pass them on to so many others. Thank God for what thanksgiving can do.

18

WHY SO MANY LOVE JESUS

Why do so many millions of people love Jesus? I do not recall ever hearing even one person speak an unkind word about Him. After some heartbreaking calamity, I have sometimes heard people express bitterness toward God. Some have felt that God was cruel and unjust because He allowed certain things to happen, and their agonizing questions of "Why?" have even caused them to feel hatred toward God. But even those people became tender in their hearts when they thought of the earthly life of Jesus.

Before He ascended into heaven, Jesus was sitting with His disciples around the fireside. They had breakfast together. Jesus turned to Simon Peter and said, "Simon, son of Jonas, lovest thou me?" Three times the Lord asked Peter that same question, and three times Peter replied, "Yea, Lord; thou knowest that I love thee" (John 21:15–17).

If at this very moment Jesus spoke to any one of us and asked, "Do you love Me?" we would say, "Yes, Lord, I do love Thee." There have been times when we have been indifferent to Him; with shame we remember times when we have been unfaithful to Him. We have not lived as He has wanted us to live, and we are not nearly as much like Him as we would like to be. Yet we do love Him.

As little children we were taught to sing:

> Jesus loves me, this I know,
> For the Bible tells me so.

That did not seem strange to us, and we loved Him in return. When finally we walk through life's last valley and our eyelids begin to close, His name will be upon our lips. It will not be difficult for us to sing:

> Jesus, Lover of my soul,
> Let me to Thy bosom fly.

There is a thrill in our hearts as we read how the first Christians loved Him. Not only did they love Him until death; they also loved Him unto death—that is, they continued to love Him even if it caused their deaths. And today there are millions of people who would suffer even the worst torture rather than denounce their love for Him. Why do people love Him so?

He Is So Lovable

One reason is that He is so lovable. Take all the qualities of character that are most attractive to us—goodness,

116

unselfishness, courage, tenderness, humility, faith—and He perfectly lived those qualities. Nobody loves selfishness; we love unselfish people. One cannot help but love Jesus because we see in Him all the things that inspire love.

He Loves Us

Another reason we love Him is because He loves us. When the young ruler approached Him, the Bible says, "Then Jesus beholding him loved him" (Mark 10:21). That can be said of every person He ever sees—even of each one of us.

A man told me recently that he had promised again and again to do the right thing, but shamefully he had failed. He asked, "Can I expect still another chance?" I quoted the words:

> Though I forget Him, and wander away,
> Still He doth love me wherever I stray.

And knowing that to be true, we still love Him.

Our Best Friend

There is another reason: we love Him because He is our best Friend.

An English publication offered a prize for the best definition of a friend. Thousands of answers were received, and the one that was given first prize was this: "A friend is the one who comes in when the whole world has gone out." That is a mighty good definition.

A young man by the name of Joseph Scriven was deeply in love with a girl. They had planned to marry, but she was accidentally drowned, and for months he was bitter and heartbroken. But as he walked through the valley of the shadow, he felt the Presence. He had a deep experience of Christ and he wrote:

> What a Friend we have in Jesus,
> All our sins and griefs to bear!

In the second verse he said:

> Can we find a friend so faithful,
> Who will all our sorrows share?
> Jesus knows our every weakness:
> Take it to the Lord in prayer.

That has become one of the best loved of all the hymns because it expresses the deep feeling of so many hearts. Jesus does come in, even when the whole world walks out. But I think there is still a better definition of a friend.

Once Henry Ford was having lunch with a man when suddenly he asked him, "Who is your best friend?" The man started naming certain people. "No," said Mr. Ford, "I will tell you who your best friend is." He took out a pencil and wrote on the tablecloth this sentence: "Your best friend is he who brings out the best that is within you."

Recall the first and the last conversations Simon Peter had with Jesus. The last time they talked together was when Jesus asked, "Simon, son of Jonas, lovest thou me . . . ?" and Simon replied, "Yea, Lord; thou knowest that I love thee." He did love Jesus, and Jesus knew it.

The main reason why Simon loved Him is seen in the first conversation they had. When Jesus saw him the first time, He said, "Thou art Simon, . . . thou shalt be called Cephas" (John 1:42); that is, "You are a weak man now, but I see possibilities of strength within you that I shall develop, and I will make of you a strong man." Peter knew how Jesus wanted to help him to be a better man, and he loved Him for it.

Jesus had a way of making people believe two things about themselves: first, "I ought not to be the way I am"; second, "I need not stay the way I am."

In each one of us there is a mixture of the best and the worst. Each human heart is an unseen battlefield where the good and the bad are fighting it out; sometimes one wins and sometimes the other wins. When the bad wins out, we are ashamed and disgusted with ourselves. But when the good wins, we have a clean feeling inside and we are filled with joy; we have proved ourselves to be real men. Jesus brings out our best, and that is another reason why we love Him so.

He Brings Out Our Best

One is reminded of an experience of Peter Marshall that illustrates how Jesus brings out the best within a man. A senator heard Peter Marshall preaching and began to fall in love with the Christ about whom Marshall preached. The senator was a timid man who had been appointed from a Western state to fill an unexpired term; he was expected to be the tool of a group of powerful and selfish men back home. He had been told that he could stay in Washington only as long as he did as he was told. He never dared have convictions of his own.

But as the senator listened that morning to Peter Marshall, he saw Jesus and began to feel a stirring within his soul. He said later to the preacher, "I'd like to be myself just once. I would like to feel the wind on my face on some high hill."

Marshall said, "The next time a moral issue arises, depend on Christ and on yourself. Vote as Christ would want you to vote, and you will feel that wind on your face."

Soon a bill came up that would have greatly benefited the group of men in the senator's home state but would have caused thousands of little people to suffer. Peter Marshall had his radio on when the roll-call vote on the bill was being taken; it was close and much depended on that senator's vote. When his name was called, there was a moment of silence; then came a thundering "No!" Marshall said to himself, "In the name of Jesus Christ he is now feeling the wind on his face."

We love Jesus because He inspires us to stand up and be our best.

A friend of mine tells the story of a couple who were poor when they married, but later they began to make money and had more of the things money can buy. Gradually their lives changed: they didn't go to church as they used to; there were more and more parties, and they got to drinking a good deal. One night they both got pretty drunk and on the way home began quarreling. As they got out of the car, they said things they wouldn't have said in sober moments. She slapped him, and then he knocked her to the ground. Suddenly he realized what he had done. He bent down to her and said, "I didn't mean that. I love you." In bewilderment she said, "What has come over us?"

Finally she said, "Maybe we ought to pray." Together they lifted their eyes to the Christ they had known since they were children. As they had drunk together, the worst had come out in them; but as they looked to Jesus, the best came out. They got a hold on themselves and on a new life; they began to be happy again.

Jesus brings out the best in each one of us when we give Him a chance. That is why so many people sing His praises.

19

WHAT MAKES A MAN GREAT?

If I were asked to name the greatest people in the Bible, Moses, David, and Paul would quickly come into my mind. Whose name would come next? I would hesitate, but only for a moment—Simon Peter would be my next name.

After naming Peter, I would stop and ask the question, "What makes a man great?" Peter did not have the opportunities of Moses, David, and Paul. The first two grew up in palaces, and all were given the advantage of the very best education; they were Ph.D's. Peter got about as far as the second grade. He was an unlearned day laborer, yet he became such a man as to be considered great. What made him great?

Courage to Dare

First, he had the courage to dare. While others were thinking it over, Peter was striking while the iron was hot. There were times when his impulsiveness got him into trouble, and he made mistakes, but no man ever does anything who never gets started.

I shall never forget the first Model T Ford we had. On cold Sunday mornings it was my job to get the car started and the engine warmed up while Papa was shaving and meditating upon his sermon. In order to get to his country church over the muddy roads, we needed an early start. I would pour hot water on the engine, jack up the rear wheel, and crank and crank and crank. Just to remember it now makes my back hurt. I was mighty happy when Papa finally got a car with a self-starter.

Peter was a man with a self-starter. One night the disciples were on board a ship during a storm, and across the water they saw what looked like a man walking toward them. It frightened them. But then a familiar voice spoke out, saying, "Be of good cheer; it is I; be not afraid." While the others were thinking, Peter answered the Lord, "If it be thou, bid me come unto thee on the water."

He didn't stop to ask if he could walk on water, or to consider the consequences if he should sink; he dared to step forward. And he did walk on the water (Matt. 14:22–29)! It is amazing what men have accomplished who have dared to try. Peter later began to sink and had to be pulled out, but even so, he got a thrill that those who stayed safely on board didn't get.

One day there was a great crowd of people mocking the first Christians. "These men are full of new wine," they said (Acts 2:13). These Christians had experienced Pentecost, but while some of them were thinking about what to do, Peter stood up and began to speak. He might have said, "I'll go home and prepare a sermon and then preach to these people"; but the crowd would have been gone. He didn't stop to ask if he had the ability to speak in public, or if he had a sermon to give; he just began talking, and that day three thousand people were converted (Acts 2:41).

Lesser people think about doing many things, but they concentrate on the difficulties instead of the possibilities until their chance is gone. Great men are not afraid to make mistakes. Great men are not afraid to fail. Great men have the courage to make up their minds and to act.

He Gave Himself to Something Greater

A second thing that made Peter great is that he found something greater than himself and unreservedly gave himself to it. No person is ever great until he loses his life for something bigger than he is. No person ever becomes great until he finds something for which he is willing to die. As long as a man holds onto himself, he never knows what greatness is. Our Lord clearly stated this principle: "For whosoever will save his life shall lose it: and whosoever will lose his life for my sake shall find it" (Matt. 16:25).

Recently I reread Roger Burlingame's biography of Henry Ford. It is fascinating to see how that frail, timid farm boy became what he did become; he hardly learned to read or write, yet he changed the industrial world. Study his life and you will see how he ceased to care what happened to Henry Ford. He lost himself in a great enterprise. So it is with every great man.

When I am traveling and people learn that I used to live in Atlanta, invariably I am asked about three people: Margaret Mitchell, Bobby Jones, and Bobby Dodd. The nation regards all three of them as great. Margaret Mitchell gave herself to the writing of a novel; Bobby Jones gave himself to the mastering of a game; Bobby Dodd has lost his life to the cause of developing character through the medium of football. No person becomes great except through the process of dedication to something bigger than himself.

Notice carefully these words: "Now as He walked by the sea of Galilee, He saw Simon and Andrew his brother casting a net into the sea: for they were fishers. And Jesus said unto them, Come ye after Me, and I will make you to become fishers of men. And straightway they forsook their nets, and followed Him" (Mark 1: 16–18). Simon Peter saw in Christ something greater than the possession of a boat. He said, "I'll give my life to Him and to what He represents." Peter turned himself loose and took hold of One who was greater. He ceased to be concerned about himself, and in the losing of his life, who can deny that he found it?

It wasn't an easy struggle for Peter. There were times when he misinterpreted Christ, but he kept working at his consecration. Years later he found himself in jail under a death sentence. Many other Christians had already been executed; James, the brother of John and one of Peter's closest friends for many years, had had his head cut off only a few days before.

Came the night before Peter was to die in the morning. What did Peter do? Become hysterical? No. He lay down and went to sleep (Acts 12:1–6). Having given himself to a greater cause, he wasn't afraid of anything that might happen to him. Had he tried to hold on to his life, he would have ended up a worried, frustrated, defeated man.

He Started Again After Failure

One of the marks of a truly great man is his willingness to start again after a failure. All great people fail. Before Edison learned to make a lightbulb, he failed nearly a thousand times. But he always came back and began anew.

Here is one of the reasons Simon Peter became great. He had left his boat to follow Jesus and had walked with the Savior to the place where they had become intimate friends. He felt sure of himself. So it came as a shock when Jesus said to the disciples, "All ye shall be offended because of me this night" (Matt. 26:31). Peter did not trust the others, but he was confident of himself. He replied to the Lord, "Though all men shall be offended because of thee, yet will I never be offended" (v. 33).

So sure of himself—though the Lord needed to pray—Peter lay down and went to sleep. He felt strong enough without seeking the help of God. Then the soldiers came to take Jesus. Did Peter run away? No. Though he was far outnumbered, he drew his sword to defend his Master. But later that night a little girl pointed her finger at him as one of Jesus' friends, and Peter lost his nerve. Often it is that a man stands courageous in the face of great danger, as Peter did in the face of a company of soldiers, and then fails in some slight stress, as Peter did at the accusation of a little girl. We let down our guard and trip over a small hurdle.

Peter did not try to excuse or justify his failure. He faced up to it honestly, was ashamed of it, wept over it, and repented. Now we see his true greatness begin to emerge. Who is the hardest person to love? Someone who has done you wrong? No. To forgive someone else makes us feel noble and big. The hardest person to love is someone we have wronged. Instead of seeking forgiveness, we want to justify ourselves and in some way put the blame on the one we have wronged. Certainly we do not want to see that person more than we must. But not Peter. When the news came that Jesus had risen, the record states that instead of sulking in some corner, "Then arose Peter, and ran unto the sepulcher" (Luke 24:12). He had failed, but he had the grace to admit it and start again.

He Was Humble

One other mark of a great man that we see in Peter is humility. Writing to those who were seeking to be Christians, Peter said, "Be clothed with humility: for God resisteth the proud, and giveth grace to the humble" (1 Peter 5:5).

There is a legend that in the face of persecution, Peter was fleeing from Rome. Outside the city he met a man carrying a cross. He did not recognize him at once and he asked, "Quo vadis" ("Where goest thou?"). The man replied, "I am going to Rome to be crucified again." Now Peter knew Him. He turned and went back into the city. He was crucified, but tradition tells us that he made only one request: that he be crucified with his head downward, for he was not worthy to be crucified in the same position as his Lord. Peter became a great man.

20

WHY JUDAS FAILED

The name "Judas" is one of the best known of Jesus' disciples, yet the man Judas is one of the least known of the Twelve. About all we know of Judas is that he betrayed his Lord. But that is not all he did.

A Man Jesus Chose

When I think of Judas, the first thing that comes to mind is that he was such a man that Jesus chose him. The night before Christ made His final selection, He went out into the mountains alone and spent all night talking to God about it (Luke 6:12). I am sure Jesus had been thinking about whom He would choose for many months; likely He had a list of forty or fifty men. One by one He eliminated names from His list until the twelve best ones were left. Judas was one of them.

Of course, Judas had some faults. Each man on the list had faults: Peter was both boastful and cowardly; Thomas was gloomy and given to doubt; James and John were selfish and overly ambitious; all the disciples would seek places of honor for themselves and would dispute with each other. But Jesus was willing to take a chance on these men. He also saw their possibilities.

Not only did Jesus have confidence in Judas, so did the others of the Twelve. They elected him treasurer of their group; they were willing to trust both his ability to handle their money and his honesty; he went on missions with the others. He must have had many fine qualities. If Jesus were here in the flesh today, I would be very pleased to know that I was as good a man as Judas so that He might choose me.

Judas Chose Jesus

Also, we need to remember that Judas chose Jesus. That says a lot about him. He is accused of being greedy and a lover of money, but he too gave up his business, his home, his friends, and all that he had to follow Jesus. We are not told the circumstances under which Jesus called him. Maybe Judas heard Jesus speak, saw Him work His miracles, watched His pure life. Something deep in Judas' heart was stirred. And when Jesus said to him, "Follow me," Judas said, "Yea."

We remember the young ruler who turned away from Christ because the price was too high. Others refused Him when He told how the foxes had holes, the birds nests, but the Son of Man nowhere to lay His head. But when the call came, Judas broke with the past and accepted the obligations of discipleship.

Before we condemn Judas, let us ask ourselves if we have done as well as he. Some may say, "I never betrayed Christ," but it may be that they have never even started with Him. Jesus' call is to every man—maybe not to leave his work, but certainly to leave his sin; maybe not to be a full-time disciple, but certainly to be a full-time Christian. Joseph of Arimathea gave his tomb for the Lord to be buried in, but he never openly declared for Christ. Judas was willing to let the world know whose side he was on. I admire him for that.

Why Did He Fail?

Judas was as sincere as any of the twelve disciples, yet he failed. Why did he act as he did? Church people need to find the answer to that question. Judas is not a sermon to preach to the strangers of Christ; Judas is a sermon for the inner circle, for the friends of Christ.

During the Last Supper Jesus said, "One of you shall betray me." The other men did not point their fingers at Judas and say, "Thou art the man"; instead they said, "Lord, is it I?" (Matt. 26:21–22). Instead of accusing another, each recognized his own weakness and danger. It is easy to condemn Judas and paint him black, but he stands as an awful warning to me and to you.

The greatest and strongest Christian who ever lived was afraid that he might follow Judas. St. Paul said, "But I keep under my body, and bring it into subjection: lest that by any means, when I have preached to others, I myself should be a castaway" (1 Cor. 9:27). It can happen to even the saintliest person in the church today.

The reason we study Judas is that we can take warning and be on guard. There are three main reasons why Judas did what he did.

1. He let himself get too interested in money. Judas had a capacity for finance. (Probably he had been in

some business where he had learned to handle money, and it was natural for the disciples to ask him to look after their finances.) Though he gave up his business for Christ, still he couldn't forget what money could do. When some poor and needy person came asking help of Jesus, it was Judas the treasurer who gave money to him. No doubt there were hundreds who thanked God in their prayers for Judas. And Judas came to like that. It gave him a sense of importance and power.

When Mary anointed the feet of the Master with the costly perfume, it was Judas who protested the waste. He said, "Why was not this ointment sold for three hundred pence, and given to the poor?" (John 12:3–5). Of course Judas would have said, "I am only interested in money for the good it can do," but money gets a strange hold on people. Jesus could see that people could be helped in ways beyond the reach of money. But Judas didn't see that. I have a feeling that Jesus looked at Judas when he said, "Take heed, and beware of covetousness: for a man's life consisteth not in the abundance of the things which he possesseth" (Luke 12:15).

There are people today who get their minds on business, salaries, houses, cars, and the things money can do to the point where they forget Christ. They give generously, they live pretty decent lives; but they don't pray as they used to, they give less and less of themselves to the church and the work of God, and gradually they depend on the power of money. And let us not smugly point our fingers at the rich. A man can be just as selfish with a dollar as he can with a million.

When I realize that money can make me a Judas, I should take warning.

2. Judas failed because of his disappointment in Christ. He believed in the power of Christ and thought He would quickly conquer the earth. Instead of conquering, Jesus seemed to be wasting His time with sick people and blind people who, according to Judas' standards, did not matter.

We recall that after Jesus fed the multitude, the people wanted to make Him a king. Instead, Jesus got away from the crowds and talked about the "bread of life." He made it clear to His disciples that His path would be one of rejection, sorrow, and death. The Bible says, "From that time many of his disciples went back, and walked no more with him." He turned to the Twelve and asked, "Will ye also go away?" Peter said, "Lord, to whom shall we go?" Jesus then said, "Have not I chosen you twelve, and one of you is a devil?" (John 6:66–70).

Jesus could see that Judas had lost faith in His plans. Some believe that in betraying Him to His enemies, Judas was trying to force the hand of Jesus; Judas never believed that Jesus lacked the power or that He would let Himself be crucified. And that is why many lose interest in Christ. They just cannot understand His methods. "Why doesn't God do something?" they impatiently ask. Because God's plan is different from their ideas, they turn away from Him.

3. Another reason why Judas betrayed Christ—perhaps the main reason—was that his pride was wounded. From the very beginning Judas was a lonely man. He came from Kerioth; he was the only one of the Twelve who was not a Galilean. He admired Christ enough to give up all he had to be with Him. It must have wounded him deeply to see Peter, James, and John enjoy a closer

friendship with the Master. He felt he did not receive the proper recognition.

It is so easy for loneliness to turn into jealousy and then into hate and then into vindictive actions. Dr. Alfred Adler tells of a little six-year-old girl who was the darling of her parents. Then another baby came into their home, and the baby began to get so much attention that the little girl couldn't stand it. One day the older sister got her chance and threw the baby into some water where she was drowned. Such a story shocks us, but it happens in many ways. Right here is the main reason for trouble in the church. How wonderful it would be if we would heed His words: "He that loseth his life for my sake shall find it" (Matt. 10:39).

Whatever the reason, the awful fact is that one who knew Christ, lived with Him day by day, ate by His side, perhaps slept under the same blanket with Him, appreciated Him so much that he left all he had to follow Him—that man betrayed Him! And if it could happen to Judas, how much easier it might happen to one of us who has not had such close contact with Him! "Lord, is it I?" is a supreme question for me—for you.

Judas betrayed Him; Peter denied Him. There wasn't much difference between the two. Yet Peter came back to Him in repentance. Judas didn't repent and found life not to be worth living. May I know that no matter what I have done, even now He will forgive me and give me a new start.

21

THE WAY
IS NARROW

In a forum for college students that I was conducting, one boy said, "My objection to religion is that it takes all the fun out of life." Some twenty-five other students in the group expressed agreement with that idea.

Young people do not like restrictions. They want to be free to do as they please. So, when religion is presented in the form of "Thou shalt not," they resent it. And, like the prodigal son, they want to get away from the disciplines and restraints and go where they can taste the full joys of life.

We know that Jesus said, "Strait is the gate, and narrow is the way, which leadeth unto life" (Matt. 7:14), and we speak of the Christian life as "the strait and narrow way." This is offensive to a lot of people. We pride ourselves on being "broad minded"; we resent being called "narrow minded." As a result, many people refuse to give Christ a chance in their lives; in fact, Jesus said that "few there be that find" the narrow way. Why do people refuse the narrow way?"

Some "Good" People Repel

One reason is some of the people who profess to walk that narrow way; instead of making goodness attractive, they have made it repellent. There are some types of "good people" we would walk blocks out of our way to avoid meeting. They are the "negatively good"; they have never done anything good, but they have kept the lid clamped so tightly on their badness that they have become dried up and sour. Then there are the "critically good"; their religion is strictly for export, to be applied to somebody else. They are always meddling with other people's lives. Then there are the "narrowly good"; they make a great to-do about insignificant matters of behavior and miss all the great issues of life that really amount to something. Believing that those types of people are Christians, it's no wonder many people are driven away from Christ. Such "good" people become an embarrassment to God's larger purposes.

Some Think Christ Was Wrong

Another reason many people refuse the "narrow way" is that they sincerely believe Christ was wrong—not that He was wrong when He implied that every person wants life, because both the good and the bad want that. Every normal person wants a life that is happy and successful. But many disagree that the way to find life is by the "narrow way."

One man complained, "Everything I like is either immoral or fattening." And vast numbers of people believe that life at its best can be found in those forbidden pleasures and in escaping those hard duties. Indeed, many do feel that religion takes all the fun out of life and, believing that, they pass it by.

Napoleon and his men were crossing a desert, and the sun beat down on those tired soldiers until they develop a burning thirst. Ahead they saw a beautiful lake, green grass, and palm trees that provided cool shade. The men shouted, broke ranks, and ran for the water. But as they ran, the lake ran ahead of them and they could never catch it. It was a mirage; it appeared to be, but it wasn't there.

In the heart of man is a thirst for life—a life that means happiness and success. Jesus said, "Narrow is the way, which leadeth unto life" (Matt. 7:14), but we allow ourselves to be fooled into thinking Jesus was wrong. Evil often promises us more pleasure than does the good. St. Paul tells us, "Satan himself is transformed into an angel of light" (2 Cor. 11:14). He surely is! No matter how we run after life in those things that are wrong, we never catch it. It is only a mirage; it never satisfies our thirst.

Why Is Anything Forbidden?

In insisting that "narrow is the way," Jesus is forbidding to us many things—but why does He forbid us anything? If something is wrong for us to do, it is wrong for one of three reasons:

1. Our doing it may do harm to some other person. Paul said, "If meat make my brother to offend, I will

eat no flesh" (1 Cor. 8:13). We are our brother's keeper, and there are some things we must deny ourselves on that account.

2. Some things are wrong because they degrade our souls—profanity, for example.

3. But most things that are wrong are wrong because they knock us out of something better. The other afternoon I was in my study preparing my sermon for the following Sunday morning. The phone rang. It was a friend inviting me to play golf. It was a beautiful day, and I needed the exercise. I would have enjoyed the game. Often it is not wrong—rather is it right—for me to play golf. But for me to have gone that day would have been very wrong. It would have meant trying to preach without adequate preparation. If I had let golf do that to me, then in that instance playing golf would have been a sin.

A mother tells a child to turn off the television set, not because the program is bad for the child. It may be a good program. But if the child needs to study his lessons, or eat his dinner, or go to bed for the proper amount of sleep, then for him to continue looking at the program becomes wrong.

"Narrow is the way," said Christ. The Christian denies himself many things simply because he has more important things to do. A Christian is not so much concerned with what is wrong as he is with what is right, and as he gives himself to the right he has no time or desire for the wrong.

Jesus said, "Narrow is the way," not because He wants to restrict us, but rather because He wants us to possess something. He said, "I am come that they might have life, and . . . have it more abundantly" (John 10:10). Life is what He wants us to have, and there is only one way for us to have it—the narrow way.

If the word "narrow" sounds offensive, then consider this thought: If we do not deny ourselves the bad life for the sake of the good life, then we must deny ourselves the good life for the sake of the bad life. You can't have both—you must deny one or the other. Either give up your bad temper for the sake of having friends, or give up friends for the sake of having a bad temper. Either give up your hate for the sake of being able to love, or give up your love for the sake of being able to hate.

Stand at a corner where two main thoroughfares of a city intersect. In the center is a traffic light that says "stop" to the cars on one street while it says "go" to the cars on the other street. Without the light there would be turmoil and congestion. You see, something must be held back in order to let something else go ahead. Some things must be controlled in order to give liberty to other things. Jesus said, "Narrow is the way," not because He wanted to deny us, but rather because He wanted us to get somewhere.

I had gone to another city for some speaking engagements, and when my work was finished I went to the airport to buy a ticket. When the man said, "Where to?" I didn't say, "I'm broad-minded—I'll go anywhere." I wanted a ticket to my home city. It was after midnight when I got there. Often I enjoy driving through the city, but that night I told the taxi driver to take the shortest distance between the airport and my home. There are many driveways on my street, but I insisted that we turn into only one. I was tired and wanted to get home. And when you have some place to go, the straight and narrow way is the one you want.

The Higher Goals

So, when our minds are fixed on reaching the high goals of life, as Jesus' mind was fixed, the narrow way becomes the most attractive. The medical student doesn't mind upwards of ten years of study because he sees something ahead. The musician doesn't mind long hours of practice because it is a means of accomplishing his purposes. The athlete gladly gives himself to hard practice and strict training because his mind is on the big game ahead.

In one of the European galleries there is a very fine statue of Apollo, a beautiful example of physical perfection. They say it is interesting to watch the crowds pass by that statue. When a person sees it, he invariably begins to straighten up. He isn't conscious of what he is doing, but seeing that statue, he wants to be like it.

That is the motive of the Christian: he sees Christ and in Christ he sees life. Seeing that, he instinctively wants to move toward it. Then it is no sacrifice to turn loose whatever may hinder him and to walk the "strait and narrow path."

John Oxenham said it well:

> To every man there openeth
> A Way, and Ways, and a Way,
> And the High Soul climbs the High Way,
> The Low Soul gropes the Low,
> And in between, on the misty flats,
> The rest drift to and fro.
> But to every man there openeth
> A High Way and a Low,
> And every man decideth
> The Way his soul shall go.

22

THE MILE THAT GETS YOU THERE

The most thrilling thing about Christianity is that it works. Take an example: Jesus said, "Whosoever shall compel thee to go a mile, go with him twain" (Matt. 5: 41). This is one of the basic laws of great living—one of the hardest to master, yet one of the most rewarding.

Jesus lived in the little country of Palestine, which had been conquered by Rome. Not only did Rome exact heavy taxes and hold those people under strict bondage, but the Romans also never let them forget they were at all times subject to their orders. This was humiliating to the people.

One of the most annoying laws was the one that allowed a Roman soldier to compel any Palestinian citizen to carry his pack for one mile. A man might be hurrying on some important mission for himself when a soldier would see him and demand, "Pick up this pack of mine and carry it a mile." He didn't ask it; he commanded it. The Jews were proud people, and you can imagine how they resented that. They would walk that mile, cursing under their breaths. Since under the law one mile was the limit a soldier could command from a person at any one time, we can feel certain they carefully counted their steps and did not go one step farther than the law demanded.

Jesus said, "Don't stop with one mile—go a second mile." People must have thought Him crazy, but He wasn't. He was giving them something to live by. The first mile was compulsory; the second mile was voluntary. The first mile one must go; the second mile one chooses to go. Jesus would have people know that living really begins after one has walked the mile of duty and then stepped out on the mile of privilege.

Eliminates the Drudgery

The second mile eliminates the drudgery of life. In one of his books William James talks about our "first layer of fatigue." We push and work to the point of exhaustion. We say, "I am so tired, I could drop." James says that most people operate within the limitation of the first fatigue. They never really accomplish much. But he explains that beyond this first fatigue there is almost inexhaustible power. He says, "The people who do great things are those who drive past this first fatigue."

Runners on a track team speak of catching their "second wind." After he has been running for a time, the runner's legs get heavy and they begin to slow down. But the runner keeps going, and suddenly he gains access to new strength. His legs are not tired any longer and he begins to breathe easier; he picks up speed.

Just as airplanes can break through the "sound barrier," so people can break through the "fatigue barrier." The point where one breaks through this barrier is that place where we begin what Jesus called "the second mile."

Many people go through life doing only those things they are compelled to do. They find life to be hard, not much joy, and they are constantly tired. Other people go beyond the call of duty and freely give themselves on a voluntary basis. They find life to be a stimulating, thrilling adventure.

Jesus divided life into two miles: the first mile is compulsion, the second is consecration. On the first mile a man is constantly demanding his "rights"; on the second mile he is constantly looking for his opportunities. The mile of duty is no fun; on the mile of consecration we find great joy.

A well-known minister recalled how his mother once sent him to pick a quart of raspberries. He despised picking raspberries, but she commanded him to do it, and he went to the patch in a rebellious mood. He resented having to live in a world where little boys had to pick berries when they wanted to play. As he picked the berries, suddenly he had an idea. It would be fun to surprise the family at dinner that night; instead of having one quart of berries, they would have two, and everyone could have an extra helping. Thinking about surprising the family, he hurriedly and happily picked the first and then the second quart, and he said he never enjoyed anything more. That is the way the second-mile principle works all the way through life. If we go beyond mere duty and compulsion, we find new strength and happiness.

The Mile of Progress

Not only does the second mile eliminate the drudgery of life; it is also the mile on which we make our progress. The man who thinks only of his duty never really has much success, but when a man thinks in terms of voluntary consecration, he gets enthusiastic. You never find enthusiasm in the things you are compelled to do, but you find enthusiasm in the things you want to do. The word "enthusiasm" is derived from the Greek words *en Theos,* meaning "in God" or "inspired by God."

I recommend to a lot of people Frank Bettger's book *How I Raised Myself from Failure to Success in Selling.* By the time he was forty years old, Frank Bettger had made enough money selling insurance so that he could retire. He says it was because of his enthusiasm. He had learned the power of enthusiasm while playing baseball.

Bettger had started out with the Johnstown team in the Three States League. He was only interested in the salary they were paying him, and he was fired after three weeks because he was so lazy. He ended up with the Chester, Pennsylvania, team at a salary only one-sixth as much as he had been getting. One day he suddenly got interested in playing the game. He began to play ball with such enthusiasm that people thought he was crazy. He was always talking it up; he never sat down on the bench between innings; he always ran instead of walking. A few months later he was playing third base for the St. Louis Cardinals.

When Bettger stopped thinking of how little he could do to collect his salary and began playing the game because he loved it, he moved from the first mile to the second, and there he found success. The principle applies to all of life.

Our Largest Rewards

Jesus said, "Whosoever shall compel thee to go a mile, go with him twain"; that is, stop rebelling against what you are compelled to do and give yourself to your larger opportunities. It is on the second mile that we gain our largest rewards.

I remember that my father used to preach often about the second mile, but all I remember about his sermons was one story he told: A man rented a house. There were no trees around it, and his wife suggested they set out some. It would have been easy to walk down to the woods, dig up a few small trees, and set them out in the yard. But he refused; he said it was his duty to pay the rent and that was all.

The years went by, but the man never set out any trees. Every month for twenty-five years he paid the rent. Then one day he bought the house and it belonged to him—but there were no trees in the yard. My father said that if the man had gone just a little beyond his duty, he would have ended up with nice trees to give him cool shade.

The second mile rewards us in our relationships with other people. As you go along through life, somebody will do you wrong. There are four attitudes you may take: (1) "If he hurts me, I will hurt him more"—that is vindictiveness; (2) "If he hurts me, I will treat him the same"—that is retribution, the old law of "an eye for an eye"; (3) "If he hurts me, I will ignore him and have nothing more to do with him"—that is disdain; (4) "If he hurts me, I will love and serve him"—that is the Christian way, and that is the way that brings rewards.

One day Jesus was nailed to a cross. He had been mistreated as no other man had been. His trials were not fair, and even as He was hanging there He was scorned and ridiculed. He had the power to strike dead every one of His persecutors or even to ignore them utterly. But He did neither; instead, He began to pray. What was His very first prayer? For the good of those who had done Him wrong. He went the second mile, and on that mile multitudes have seen Him as the Savior. He bore His cross of duty, but He went further, and in doing so He gained His greatest reward.

A man moved into a house next door to a friend of mine. After a few days, the new neighbor phoned my friend angrily to tell him that his driveway was two feet over their line. He demanded that they employ a surveyor. My friend said, "We do not need a surveyor. You go out and set some stakes where the line should be, and I'll move my driveway. I'll accept your judgment in the matter."

He didn't hear any more from the neighbor for several days and neither did he see any stakes. One day they met in the yard, and my friend asked about the line. The neighbor said, "Oh, forget the line. There is enough for both of us, and two feet one way or the other makes no difference." My friend went the second mile, and in so doing he won the friendship of a neighbor.

23

THE PLACE NAMED HEAVEN

"I go to prepare a place for you," said Jesus (John 14:2). Underscore that word *place*. Before God made people, He made a place for them to live. He anticipated all the needs of mankind, and He took care of those needs in the creation of this world.

God knew that man's body would require food; so He created soil in which things could grow. Man can appreciate beauty; so there are majestic mountains, colorful birds, precious stones, lovely flowers, blue skies, and so much else. Man needs to satisfy his spirit of adventure, so God made a big world in which man could roam and explore.

In the world God hid many things for man to search out. It was thousands of years before the source of electricity was discovered. Not very long ago we learned of the power within the atom and how to release it. Man discovered how to send sound through the air, and then pictures, and now we have radio and television.

To live on earth, man needs lots of water. His fields must be watered or nothing will grow. He needs water to drink and to bathe in. God worked out for man the finest water system that can be imagined: the oceans are the giant reservoirs; the sun draws the water up into the clouds, and the winds blow the clouds over the earth, and the rain falls; the water serves its purposes and then returns to the ocean. In the process it is purified and the same water can be used over and over again.

What a wonderful world God has prepared for us! Yet it contains many challenges for man, and in meeting these challenges man develops himself. There are illnesses in the earth, too. I do not know why God included in the world the possibilities of yellow fever, polio, cancer, and so many other diseases. But little by little man is learning to overcome these enemies of his body. Someday man will even learn how to cope with cyclones and hurricanes.

God did not fix it so that one is born with knowledge. Instead, He gave men minds that can think and study, learn and remember. He made a world in which there is plenty to do, and through the meeting of the challenges and opportunities of this life, man develops himself and grows in character and inner strength.

God arranged it so that on this earth we would live as families. We would come to love each other. In His plan, men work together, have fellowship with one another, the strong helping the weak. We belong to each other. We would miss so much if we did not have human friendships and associations. Parents nurture and care for the little ones. Teachers impart their knowledge and help others to learn. In so many ways do we serve each other.

In this world we grow as individuals. We are born as babies and become men and women. We also grow as a people; each generation moves a bit higher in the scale of living. From all this we can know something about the place prepared for man beyond this world. I think heaven is the way it is here—only more so.

A Place to Grow

What kind of place is heaven? Judging from the kind of place God made for us here, and judging from what we know about Christ, we can pretty well know some things about heaven.

Jesus said, "I go to prepare a place for you." Surely heaven is a place where we can continue to grow and develop. Jesus was a Teacher here on earth; surely He is the same in the Father's house. The Bible says, "Now we see through a glass, darkly" (1 Cor. 13:12); that is, there is so much that is dim to us. But there we will see and understand so much more—we will continue to grow in grace and advance in knowledge.

Some people think that heaven is a place where we will find eternal rest. But the idea of resting forever does not seem very exciting to me. For many it will be a blessed relief to be rid of their old, tired, patched-up, and pain-ridden bodies. But the Bible promises that in heaven we will be given a new body with which we can accomplish more.

There is a lovely verse in Revelation that says, "Blessed are the dead which die in the Lord from henceforth: Yea, saith the Spirit, that they may rest from their labours; and their works do follow them" (14:13). The key words in that verse are "labours" and "works." Here the word "labours" means weariness, suffering, exhaustion; the word "works" means results achieved and abilities that are acquired. Our wearisome burdens will be left behind; our abilities and capacities will be kept and developed.

Speaking of heaven, the Bible says, "His servants shall serve him" (Rev. 22:3). I do not know exactly what type of work we will do, but I do know it will be in God's service, and that is the best work of all. Here we are so handicapped; there we will have both the abilities and the opportunities to do our best. The next life will be filled with exciting activity.

Know One Another

In heaven we will be the same people as we are here. Our personal identities will survive. Many things about you will survive death—your temperament, your abilities, your personality. If you know someone here, you will know him when you meet him there. But fellowship one with another will be on a different basis in the next life.

Here we do not really know each other. We are too hurried to get acquainted, and we are not even capable of really knowing ourselves. After some shameful action we say, "I don't know why I did that"—and we don't. Certainly we are not capable of judging others here.

On the other side of life the veil will be lifted, and because we will know each other and understand, we will be kinder and more patient. We will love more completely and more creatively. There we will mean more to one another. Here we are separated by class and color and creed; there we will all simply be children of God.

There are many people on this earth whom I admire but whom I have never had a chance to know. I am disappointed that I never got to see President Franklin Roosevelt. There are many others I could name. I would like to talk with Abraham Lincoln, with St. Paul, David, and many others I could name. In the next life I will have that privilege. There I will see again and love again those who have gone on before me. We have not lost our loved ones who have died.

Best of all, we will see God face to face. The very thought of being in God's presence is awe-inspiring. There are many things I want to talk with God about. There I can do it.

Redemption Made Complete

Not only is heaven a place where we can work and grow and be useful, and not only will we have real and complete fellowship one with another and with God; also it is a place where our redemption will be made complete. Here we have a hard time with ourselves. We do things we should not do, and we fail to do much that we should. We feel shame and remorse, our consciences hurt, and we are so often miserably defeated. There God's redemptive love and power will complete our development.

As I have studied God's Word, I have come to realize that there will be differences in our rewards in the next life. We will not find monotonous uniformity or commonplace equality there.

The Bible very clearly teaches that there will be justice in the next life. There will be punishment for sin, but I am sure that heavenly justice will be for the purpose of redemption rather than vengeance. Surely it is as Whittier wrote:

> I know not where His islands lift
> Their fronded palms in air;
> I only know I cannot drift
> Beyond His love and care.

There is so much about the next life that no one knows. But we do know the most important thing: we enter heaven not because of any good works or merit of ours; we enter it through the merits of Jesus Christ alone and through the salvation purchased by His blood. After we have done our best, we can only say:

> In my hand no price I bring;
> Simply to Thy cross I cling.

We remember that He promised, "Because I live, ye shall live also" (John 14:19). The details of the next life are hidden from us. But we are sure it is there, and as Richard Baxter said, " 'Tis enough that Christ knows all, and I shall be with him."

24

SPEAK ALL THE WORDS OF LIFE

In the Book of Acts we read that the apostles were seized and locked in prison. But that night an angel came and opened the doors. Then the angel said to the apostles: "Go, stand and speak in the temple to the people all the words of this life" (Acts 5:17–20).

Speak "all the words," the angel said. In all the professions we see a trend toward specialization. One physician treats the eyes, another practices only surgery, another confines himself to internal medicine, and so on. Lawyers specialize, too; one tries criminal cases, another works only on tax cases, some give all their time to title work, and so on. In the days of the one-room school, the teacher taught all the subjects, but today many teachers specialize in one field.

And it is a temptation for the Christian to specialize on one part of the gospel to the neglect of the entire gospel. But "all the words" of the gospel are of equal importance and must be proclaimed.

Social Justice

There are the great social issues of the day, and justice to all peoples is one of the words of the gospel. In the first book of the Bible we are taught that we are our brother's keeper and that whatever harms one of God's children is wrong. Today the preacher is compelled to speak about such things as liquor, gambling, racial intolerance, housing conditions, indecent literature, and many other social issues. But social justice is only one of the words of the gospel.

Personal Redemption

Personal redemption is another word of the gospel. Man is an emotional creature, subject to fear, worry, and defeat. Again and again Christ spoke words of peace to troubled minds; He brought faith to fearful men and spoke to those who were defeated, inspiring them to new life. This personal gospel has been criticized by some, but nowhere in the New Testament do I find it taught that there is virtue in failure. The gospel does teach men the ways of successful living.

Also, the gospel is redemptive in that it presents a Savior from sin. For the preacher to tell man merely that he is a sinner and to condemn his sin is not preaching the "words of life"; rather is he preaching the words of death. When man becomes burdened by guilt, despair, and shame, there is a "word of life" that he should have preached to him. It is about Him whose blood cleanses from all sin, about the Christ who has the power to overcome our weaknesses and who loves us in spite of what we may have done.

Comfort

"Comfort ye, comfort ye my people," the Lord said to the prophet Isaiah (40:1). "Comfort" is one of the words of the gospel. A professor I knew in theology school used to say to his students, "In your congregation there will be broken hearts—always have a word for them."

People can be hurt in so many ways. Death takes away one we love more than we love our own selves; the prizes sought in life can be snatched away, and disappointment may forever remain in our hearts; the human body can be made to suffer pain, and doubt can weigh heavily on the mind. For so many reasons does the minister need to speak words such as: "Let not your heart be troubled: ye believe in God, believe also in me. In my Father's house are many mansions" (John 14:1–2); "Yea, though I walk through the valley of the shadow of death, I will fear no evil: for thou art with me" (Ps. 23:4); "Be still, and know that I am God" (Ps. 46:10); and "God shall wipe away all tears from their eyes" (Rev. 7:17).

Speaking of comfort, it also includes compassion. David Smith, speaking of that person we refer to as a "crank," said that if we knew all the circumstances that have warped the mind of a crank, we would see that he is like a wounded animal. He doesn't need attacking; he needs loving. So often "cranks" are people who have never learned to love because they have never received love. They are part of the crowd, but have been left out of the fellowship. The gospel challenges us to love even those who seem to be unlovable.

Stewardship

Stewardship is another one of the words of life because man must be aware of his responsibilities. Several have used the illustration of parking in a space where there was time left on the meter. (Today one is lucky to find a parking space at all, and to find one with time on the meter rarely happens.) Even if we could, we would not want to go through life parking on somebody else's nickel. Yet, many people do just that—they do not carry their full share in the support of the church and of the good causes of society.

Money and giving are not the most popular subjects a preacher can talk about, but they are among the most needful. When a society spends ten times as much in beauty parlors as it does on building the kingdom of God, something is wrong. Man is held accountable to God for his possessions. The Bible asks, "Will a man rob God?" (Mal. 3:8); and the answer is, man can and man does. The preacher who does not warn the people about their responsibility to God with their money and possessions is not preaching all the words of the gospel.

Outreach

When the angel told the apostles to speak "all the words of life," I am sure that one of the words meant to be spoken was the word "outreach." It may be called evangelism or missions—whatever the word used, the Christian faith is constantly reaching out.

My good friend, Dr. William H. Dickinson, made one of the parables of Jesus to read thus:

There was a church that grew to large numbers, and the people said to themselves, "What shall we do, for we have no room for our children or for those who wish to worship with us? This we will do. We will build greater buildings, so that our children can receive a religious education and people who have never known Christ can be invited into our fellowship. And we will say to our souls, 'Soul, thou hast a great church that will be adequate for many years. Take thine ease.'" But God said to them, "Fools, this night your souls will be required of thee!" Thus it is with any church when it becomes satisfied.

The Christian must follow the example of the shepherd who went after the last sheep that was lost. Bishop Arthur J. Moore said it well: "Evangelism is not the only business of the church, but it is the main business of the church."

Judgment

Another one of the words that the minister must speak is "judgment." That is not a pleasant word to speak; we prefer that it be omitted. But the fact of the judgment is real, and men should be told about it. It is a word that reveals the shallowness of our faith; it measures the limits of our devotion. A minister may say only those things that are pleasing to hear, but if he does he eventually comes to hate himself. And eventually his own people have contempt for him.

God is a God of judgment. In *Les Miserables* Victor Hugo asks whether it would have been possible for Napoleon to have won the battle of Waterloo. "No," he answers. "Why? On account of Wellington, on account of Blucher? No. On account of God. . . . The hour had come for supreme incorruptible justice to take notice. Napoleon had been denounced in the Infinite, and his downfall had been determined. He was obstructing God."

Anne of Austria said to Richelieu: "My Lord Cardinal, God does not pay at the end of every week, but at the end He pays."

We can go on leaving God out, disobeying His laws, failing in our duty to Him. But let us remember these words from the Bible: "Be not deceived; God is not mocked: for whatsoever a man soweth, that shall he also reap" (Gal. 6:7).

Mercy

Along with the word "justice," let the preacher also speak the word "mercy." All of us are sinners; all have fallen short. But those who turn unto the Lord will find mercy—forgiving, loving, saving mercy—waiting for them. Mercy, too, is one of the words of life.